TESSA RANSFORD was born in India, ⟨ her adult life in Scotland apart fron in the 1960s. She has published 16 the mid-70s and had poems transl Austria, France, Italy, Denmark and Poetry Library in 1984 and was director there until its establishment in new premises in 1999. She has an honorary degree for Services to Scottish Literature from the University of Paisley and in 2000 she was awarded an OBE for her services to the SPL. A Society of Authors Travelling scholarship in 2001 allowed her to produce a book of translations of poets from the Leipzig area. Tessa was founder/organiser of the School of Poets poetry workshop (1981–99) and editor of *Lines Review* poetry magazine (1988–98). Founder of the Callum Macdonald Memorial Award for Scottish pamphlet poetry in 2001 and active in Scottish PEN, she has also worked as Royal Literary Fund Writing Fellow at the Centre for Human Ecology and recently at Queen Margaret University.

Praise for Tessa Ransford's poetry:

Her poetry has 'a form of introspection almost mystical in intensity' yet with 'an intellectual control of the mind in repose . . . combining knowledge with experience'. TREVOR ROYLE ON POETRY NOW, RADIO 3

On *Light of the Mind* (winner of a Scottish Arts Council Book Award) *This is a remarkably good volume of poems, in the broadest sense religious, often mystical, accomplished in technique, clear and incisive in impression. For their stature they depend not on richness of ambiguity, but on chiseled phrasing, breadth of implication, perennial truth of subject matter.* PETER MALEKIN IN *THE TEILHARD (DE CHARDIN) REVIEW*

On *Shadows from the Greater Hill* *I have unearthed comparable pleasures only in Stevenson's Picturesque Old Edinburgh. Nothing else gets close. The book's charm is a federation of simplicities.* JAMES CRUMLEY IN *EDINBURGH EVENING NEWS*

On *A Dancing Innocence* *Like Rilke, on whom she comments in her 'Annunciations', she is drawn to the light 'with its source in daily things'; her poetry is full of rocks and water, flowers. The power of the earthly, the elemental, is set beside the power of art which 'by its rays makes our days but passing shades' as much as any sun, and the book's own patterned dance leads steadily to a union of the elemental, the aesthetic and the spiritual.* ALI SMITH

On *Seven Valleys* *Tessa Ransford's Seven Valleys has an intellectual stringency mellowed by a finely tuned ear for rhythm and cadence.* HAYDEN MURPHY IN THE *TIMES EDUCATIONAL SUPPLEMENT*

On *Medusa Dozen and other poems*
The sense you are left with after reading Medusa Dozen *is that of the enlightened mind at work, at both art and the problems of the world, rich with native wit, keen to connect and transform.* ALI SMITH IN CENCRASTUS NO 56

On *When it Works it Feels like Play*
A volume filled with carefully crafted passion, with real art and thought and questing intelligence, verse well beyond facile or fashionable word-play: poetry that matters. CATHERINE LOCKERBIE IN *THE SCOTSMAN*

By the same author

Poetry of Persons, Quarto Press 1976
While it is yet Day, Quarto Press 1977
Light of the Mind, Ramsay Head Press 1980
Fools and Angels, Ramsay Head Press 1984
Shadows from the Greater Hill, Ramsay Head Press 1987
A Dancing Innocence, Macdonald Publishers, 1988
Seven Valleys, Ramsay Head Press 1991
Medusa Dozen and Other Poems, Ramsay Head Press 1994
Scottish Selection, Akros Publications 1998 (reissued 2001)
When it works it feels like Play, Ramsay Head Press 1998
Indian Selection, Akros Publications 2000
Natural Selection, Akros Publications 2001
Noteworthy Selection, Akros Publications 2002
The Nightingale Question, Shearsman Books 2004
Shades of Green, Akros Publications 2005
Sonnet Selection with eight Rilke lyrics translated Akros Publications 2007
Truth and Beauty, Continuing Enlightenment in Scotland, Netherbow
    Chapbooks 2008

Not Just Moonshine

New and Selected Poems

TESSA RANSFORD

Luath Press Limited

EDINBURGH

www.luath.co.uk

First published 2008

ISBN (10): 1-906307-77-6
ISBN (13): 978-1-906307-77-6

The paper used in this book is recyclable. It is made from
low chlorine pulps produced in a low energy, low emission
manner from renewable forests.

The publisher acknowledges subsidy from

Scottish
Arts Council

towards the publication of this volume.

Printed and bound by
Bell & Bain Ltd., Glasgow

Typeset in 10.5 point Sabon
by 3btype.com

Contents

POEMS WRITTEN IN THE 1980S

POEMS WRITTEN IN THE 1990S

POEMS WRITTEN SINCE THE MILLENNIUM

We shall never learn to feel and respect our real calling and destiny, unless we have taught ourselves to consider everything as moonshine, compared with the education of the heart.

SIR WALTER SCOTT

Moonlight over Arthur's Seat

Tonight the mountain has laid aside solidity:
    earth that has jutted and cragged its way into sky
with trapped molten intensities pushed to their utmost reach
    then cooled and folded, crumpled into shadows

Those massive columns now dissolve again in light
    wanly drawn about their huge shoulders
concentrated in an act of illumination
    with here and there a shaded boundary

Such exchange of substance noiselessly continues
    comprehends each separate, weightless leaf
each sweep of wilderness, each casual broken stone
    that shiningly betrays the eyes of gods

From their intimate gaze we seek a sheen of protection
    yet as they probe our levels of hidden light
we wager another moment towards our destiny
    and wrap ourselves in the sleep of our own courage

Acknowledgements

Apart from poems selected from the author's previous publications, also to be acknowledged are the following magazines and anthologies in which poems have appeared (some in more than one issue) since the millennium:

The Herald; *The Scotsman*; *Scottish Review of Books*; *Markings*; *Zed 2 0*; *Fras*; *Poetry Ireland*; *Chapman*; *The Dark Horse*; *The Red Wheelbarrow*; *The Eildon Tree*; *Fife Lines*; *Textualities*; *InScotland*; *Sons of Camus Journal*; *Without Day*; *The Order of Things*; *Atoms of Delight*; *The thing that mattered most*; *Exile* (Nomad); *Between*; *60/60* (daemon); *Scottish Poems* (Macmillan children's books); *The Edinburgh Book of Scottish Poetry*; *Scottish Literature in the Twentieth Century*; *Modern Scottish Women Poets*; *Handfast*; *Handsel*; *The Luckenbooth*; *Skein of Geese* (Stanza); *100 Favourite Scottish Poems*; *100 Favourite Scottish Poems to Read Out Loud*; *Ostragehege* (Germany); CDs – *The Jewel Box*; *Writeability*; SAC Poem of the Month; video – *Pamphlet power poet power*.

Foreword

FOR TESSA RANSFORD, 'the nature of a poem is to transform or distil the material of experience inner and outer.' This work represents such distillations or transformations from the last four decades, and many of these poems have been published in previous books and pamphlets, in magazines and anthologies. Chosen and arranged according to date of composition, rather than the year in which they were published, these poems can be seen to refer more to her life than to her books. Nevertheless, *Not Just Moonshine* amounts to a small but important selection from the pool of her poems and leaves out her translations, poem-sequences, and most longer poems. The poem-books *Shadows from the Greater Hill*, a series of love/nature-songs remarkable for their quiet intensity, and the philosophical *Seven Valleys* could only be fractionally represented. Her book of translations from former East German poets, *The Nightingale Question*, her translations of Rilke, Hölderlin, and Goethe, and those from the Arabic of the Palestinian poet Iyad Hayatleh, now living in Scotland, could not be included.

Not Just Moonshine also reflects how Ransford's work has evolved over four decades: the lyricism of the deeply personal early poems is still in evidence, though her work has become more markedly engaged, and she continues to express her concerns for nature, for social justice, and for her belief in the inherent dignity of the individual. In recent poems, Ransford regards herself as seeking to learn or even unlearn, and to 'walk more lightly'.

A formalist in her writing, Ransford is not afraid of sometimes using often highly complex verse forms. Influenced by

German Romantic poetry and the tradition of *dichten und denken* – poetry and thought – Ransford is conscious of her literary and philosophical debts, and in '*Epistle*' pays tribute to those poetic teachers and mentors, 'whose lives have spoken/beyond their lives': G.M. Hopkins, Tagore, John MacMurray, George Fox, Teilhard de Chardin, Soljhenitsyn, Dame Julian of Norwich, Simone Weil, Homer, and Keats. Other influences are Rilke, Patrick Geddes, and David Jones. Elsewhere in Ransford's work, most particularly in those poems which can be said to possess a spiritual dimension, one hears echoes of the devotional poetry of the 17th-century mystics George Herbert, Henry Vaughan, and Thomas Traherne; and also of Emily Dickinson, Christina Rosetti, Alice Meynell, and Elizabeth Jennings. Yet, the label of 'Christian' poet is too restrictive for Ransford: for many years her work has reflected her openness to the values inherent in especially the mysticism of other world religions, experiences she first encountered in her childhood India.

The title of this volume 'is in defiance of the pert modernism which looks on the moon as old-fashioned.' Tessa Ransford recalls being 'enchanted by the moon's path of silver over the sea from at least the age of six, when I began to write my first poems, one called 'The Moonpath'. Something more transient yet also more eternal than the moonpath would be hard to find. I have sought understanding and synthesis in my life through the making of poetry, but I have also sought to live my life in the service of poetry. I hope that my life and poetry are integrated in a complementary whole.' The expression of this belief in complementarity and the co-inherent – 'the way in which everything is always interdependent' – is a distinctive feature of her work.

When Tessa Ransford began to emerge as a poet in the 1970s,

it was as one of very few women poets writing and being published in Scotland at that time. And of lasting significance are the openings she made for a younger generation of Scottish poets, women and men. Equally significant is the publication of *Not Just Moonshine*. Though largely retrospective, it also looks forward: to those readers coming to Ransford's work for the first time, and who too will be 'crossing the threshold/into time made new.'

Michael Lister

Poems written
in the 1970s

Poetry of persons

We love each other utterly
in sharing what we do not have;
we find each other finally
in losing what we cannot save.

We keep each other continually
in taking what we dare not hold;
we win each other daringly
when every treasure has been sold.

We fill each other with good things
when we hunger for the least
and receive the cup of blessing
uninvited to the feast.

We bring each other healing
in the strong herbs of silence;
we hear each other speaking
in the quiet voice of distance.

We come to know each other
accepting what we do not know;
we come to choose each other
whom we'd chosen long ago.

We see each other perfectly
in the beholding of the night;
we trust each other lastingly
in the unfolding of the light.

We complete each other constantly
but grow to a new whole;
we form a part of all that is
and all that is forms us a soul.

We love each other utterly
in sharing what we do not have;
we gather again abundantly
after the casting in the grave.

Platonic soul study

the amorousnesse of an harmonious soule

DONNE

The Greeks maintained no celibacy of soul
but harnessed steeds as for a chariot race
with charioteer, as an harmonious whole:

two or five together keeping pace
neck by neck and flaring nostrils wide
cornering with swift and skilful grace.

Patroclus and his horses, gentle-eyed,
drove to a death intended for another
to rally those who feared or turned aside,

yet his stallions mourned him as a brother –
so fled my soul when all its reins were loose,
the horses rearing on without a driver.

The battle lasted years, no lull, no truce,
when my soul-steeds could find no part to play,
bereft of charioteer they were no use:

sunk beneath the sea in bronze he lay
until dredged up and set upon his feet,
and prized in the museum on display.

Straight and stiff his tunic's flowing pleat,
hard the curve of rein in broken hand
with white and glassy eyes for counterfeit.

Gone his steeds that galloped on the strand –
and souls live not by charioteer alone
but harmonised, obeying love's command:

driver, wheels and horses, three in one,
mind and matter moved with energy
another circuit valiantly begun,

achieving with consummate artistry
cosmic order, virtue, passion, power,
an excellence of love most real and rare.

The world that Jack built

written to support the Scottish campaign to resist the nuclear menace – SCRAM – at the time of the building of Torness; and to support the campaign in Galloway against nuclear dumping in the hills of Mullwharchar

This is Jack who said 'I'm alright,
nuclear power makes the future bright:
this is the world I want to build
(even if everyone is killed).
It's based on uranium 235
the kind that is radioactive.'

These are the lands for which nations fight
to conquer, destroy and claim the right
to mine uranium 235
the kind that is radioactive.

These are the miners exposed to cancer
who work for those who destroy and conquer
to mine uranium 235
the kind that is radioactive.

Here are the scientists who split the atom
that splits the earth from top to bottom
who gave the secret to men of power
who bombed Japan to end the war
then made H bombs in competition
with every other western nation
as well as so-called peaceful uses –
safe industrial excuses
leading towards a nuclear world
that Jack insists he wants to build
(even if everyone is killed)
based on uranium 235
the kind that is radioactive.

Here are responsible business men
whose several profits stand to gain
from selling magic nuclear power,
safe and clean and not-for-war,
to peoples living near starvation
unclued-up in radiation;
far more energy than needed,
deadly waste that lies unheeded
and plenty of spare plutonium
to put together a little bomb –
a bomb whose possibility threatens
life-on-earth for generations.

Is this the world Jack wants to build
(even if everyone is killed)?

This is the huge enrichment plant
that feeds the fuel conversion plant
that feeds the latest new reactor
that feeds the waste re-processor
and all is repeated
until completed
except for more than a little waste
that hasn't finally been placed,
but Jack is sure that he's alright
and nuclear power makes the future bright.

Here's the 'consumer'
who pays for disaster
lives in danger
of leakage or failure
sudden death
or unexplained cancer
and whoever becomes a father or mother
fears the child may be born a monster.

This is the lorry driven for miles
to carry plutonium without any spills;
this is the ship that cannot be wrecked
and the aeroplane the 'gods' protect
because Jack thinks that he's alright
and nuclear power makes the future bright
with far more energy than we need
feeding the 'progress' that we feed;
and Jack is sure he has to build
a really progressive nuclear world
(even if everyone is killed).

And here the disused power station
untouchable with radiation
dumped upon the land we leave
to our children with our love;
while underground
and all around
liquid, solid nuclear waste
that hasn't finally been placed
slowly poisons the whole world –
the one that Jack intends to build
(even if everyone is killed)
based on uranium 235
the kind that is radioactive.

Here are the military police
whose vigilance must never cease
to keep plutonium from the fists
of unscrupulous terrorists,
who might not bother
about the future
whether it's bright
and Jack alright,
who might corrupt the armed police
whose vigilance must never cease
so that Jack can live in peace
in the world he wants to build
(even if everyone is killed)
based on uranium 235
the kind that is radioactive.

This is the human whose tiny error
plunged the world into death and terror

The end of the world that...

With gratitude to India

I was a baby in India
born among dark eyes and thin limbs
handled by slim fingers
bounced by bangles
and held high among the turbans,
surrounded by the light sari
black knot of hair
suggestion of spice,
wrapped up only by those songs
that spiral the spirit out of the dust
and lay it down again to sleep.

I crawled among bright toenails
ticked off ants by the gross
or touched the lizard in his cold quickness;
toddled past wilting bougainvillaea
to watch hoopoos on the mai-dan,
caught flashes of minivet, oriole and bulbul
and peered up into huge flowers
on tree after tree
as I broke into their shade.

Never left with a strange
babysitter
I was part of the parties, parades,
the bazaar,
could swallow the stenches and listen
to the poetry of bargaining;
heart's desire was to drink cool water
or chew a sugar-cane
and flap off the flies.

I had dysentery, sickness, paleness
boiled buffalo milk,
no welfare vitamins, no plastic pants.
The sun was a fiend, the rain was a friend
the stars only just out of reach.

Expressions were always changing:
a smile latent in sorrow
and a love in anger;
tears happened with laughter
but patience presided over every mood.

To have first found the world
in abundant India
is my life's greatest privilege.

Winter sunrise in Edinburgh

The huge pale sun behind the Braid Hills
rising
glints on the city in wands of slanting light

The threadbare half-moon hangs above
Corstorphine
where winter branches stretch and silhouette

With sunrise in her hair the girl Queen
Mary
rode to dying Darnley out at Kirk o' Field

On such a frosty forenoon Cockburn left
the lawcourts
experienced the New Town, memorised the Old

Singing a cold cadence Fergusson
the poet
shivered down the Canongate with rhythm in his feet

And citizens of Edinburgh on this very
morning
set to partners, join hands and skip down the street

TESSA RANSFORD

Craighouse hill above Edinburgh

on a sunny day in a gale

On Craiglockhart side
trees go mad
in the wind
elm, beech, oak
bellowing, berserk
root-bound

The castle giants
in cries of defiance
at the gales
in turret and tower
the wind pitches higher
brinks and fails

The silent inside
might well be afraid
of the wind
but their minds are one
with wind water, sun,
make no sound

Great walls on the hill
keep the mentally ill
from the storm
the roots of trees
keep them in one place
safe from harm.

Our rootless minds
are whirling winds
inside walls

Schooled by wind
standing their ground
city halls
of Edinburgh, straight,
are polished, upright
on parade

but the trees on the hill
are shouting the drill
and are mad

Incantation 1

Not this sinking of the sun
in livid clouds
at Arisaig,
nor the darkly-gentian sea
and eagle-headed
Sgurr of Eigg

Not the flowing cormorant
from wave of sky
to cloud of sea,
nor the splashes of white sand
in rock black
severity

Not the salmon-yellow shells
sipped in and out
the shining tide,
nor the mauve and tawny flowers
wind-washed
on the mountainside –

These are blessings for the sense
but inwardly
I turn toward
people through the centuries here
sea-worn
rock-hard

Battered between land and sea
harvested
by sword and fire,
the legends of their tragedy
loom like islands
faint, now clear

Now as the sun suffuses all
in golden blood
and swords of light
I pledge my feeble watching love
to those whose lives
are here by right

How things happen

Our meeting was beyond analysis
it happened
like sunlight catching a seagull
two seagulls
so that they fly in the gleam of it.

We were going the same way
as it happened
although we did not stop to ask
nor did we
think of going separately.

We were hoping the same world
would happen
though we did not compare notes
try to define
the method or the end of it.

We did not think of love.
If it happens
it will be beyond analysis
like two seagulls
caught in a shaft of sun.

Dunvegan, Isle of Skye

the castle seen from across the loch at sunset

dying sunlight on Dunvegan
captured from the pale horizon

craven rocks around and moorlands
callous waters of the islands

bright the wing of boat and bird
golden seaweed, fling of cloud

between the hidden Hebrides
and the Cuillins, *Eumenides*

nothing sudden here nor violent
non-committal here and silent

deep the rift of land and heart
sealed with mist all love and hurt

accomplished now the heron's flight
posed and poised for the twilight

croaking takes up his position
we who come will ask no question

Dunvegan now with folded wing
watches its own voyaging

In the fishmongers

All over the fish
and the knife that continues to work
and the marble slab
and her own red hands
the tears flow salt
like a sauce.

How is it the squared body trembles
the dark head buries its raw nose
and starting eyes
in a rough roller towel?

Has she no escape
from this catch?
Must the knife continue to clean out
guts, bones, brains
until filleted
of emotion and female pride,
flat, cold on the slab
she can cease to weep and tremble?

Mother forgive

I am a mother
and because a mother, mainly and most of me
always a mother.

Vigil I keep
against the hurt of children
and now for a lass dead in Belfast
ten years old and grown all-girl
with freckles clustered round expectant eyes.

Holy innocents
and another Rachel flung abruptly into mourning.
Do not offer comfort
there is none
none
for the children are not –
an amputation with no sealing of the flesh
no ending to the motherhood.

Girls have been killed by *homo fanaticus*:
Iphigenia sacrificed to the winds of change,
Jephthah's spontaneous daughter
caught in a web of religious observance,
and Anne Frank
chosen among the chosen
blessed among virgins
as she wrote her daily *magnificat*.

This girl was blown to bits for nothing
and we all, the very heartland of us
ancient shrine and city centre of us
all that grows *sapiens* of us
shattered with her.
We choose extinction in killing our children
when even Rachel's sobs will slowly cease.

Little girl
for you and your ten years of little womanhood
our grief is such to close the very womb –
barrenness is all.
The man-made tree stands with stark arms spread;
(do we think we know what we are doing?)
upon it, votive, I hang this bitter verse
saying
mother forgive?

Western purdah

She is veiled in children:
no-one can see her.

Her eyes reconnoitre
through the grille of twisting, childish fingers;
delicate sandals walk the path of wifeliness;
hands emerge, ringed in capable motherhood.

Folds of material hide her:
on one side those she fetches for lunch,
on the other those she carries in the evening;
the morning is pleated with housework
and covers thickly her whole back.
Head and neck are invisible,
swathed in all the times she can't recount
what she was doing.

No-one can find her:
lovers cannot reach
nor statistics pry into;
committees cannot drag her out
nor friends fuss around;
relations do not stay long;
the burquah is ready at night
to put on like a dressing-gown
whenever someone wakes.

Terribly now, after twenty years,
the purdah is removed in sudden gashes;
for the first time she is uncovered
when youth has withered.

But Allah is merciful even to western mothers:
age itself will conceal us
until we take the ultimate veil.

Hospitalisation

Illness tossed you over the rails
of our world.
The huge hospital swallowed you
then swam away
to go through its routines with you
deep and distant.

I could no more than paddle in
that element
but came often to watch from the shore
and scan the surface.

After a secret number of days
and hidden nights,
after fathomless hours enclosed
in the whale's belly
floating on tides of attention
and murmurs of movement,
the hospital will spit you out again
at my feet.

The sand is suddenly swept with
scuttling pebbles
sprays of scum and shells
as you come up on it.
I begin to lead you home, only
to discover
we are on a foreign shore.

The Yoke

A piece of wood I found, arched into a yoke
and trying felt it fitted to my neck
straitly across my shoulders, each end lying easy,
misshapen to my shape and formed for me.

Following a path that led me through a wood
I climbed towards open hill and sky
where larks ascending, burns descending harmonised
with solo call of curlew to my soul.

Casually I stooped my neck beneath the yoke –
(a poet's burden surely is but light?)
but to my load was added those of other folk
whose lot I enter into when I write:
the varied, cruel yokes, ill-fitting, ill-contrived
beneath which we have laboured in our land.

Then I knew that lightly I had taken up
no yoke but cross-beam of a crucifix,
a weight for stumbling under, *dolorosa via*,
and no Cyrenian I, no Galilean.

Woman

Woman is
acute angles of feeling
wires exposed to the world
connected at the womb

Wild circuit
sending charges through
the reasoned running of mankind
which seizes up and shocks

Woman –
suffering senses dealing
bold news; expectant limbs
receive, baptise, fulfil

She is where
all things are made new
flow of blood and water
birth of God

Rembrandt

Homer: blind, envisioned
Peter: flare-struck, fear-stricken
Jeremiah: bathed in lamentation

Here glory slanting
upon Simeon in song
or the cradled Saviour

There the questing question
in bewildered eyes
corrupted flesh
seeing just beyond its own perimeter

How long the night watch
bearing torches
gleaming?
How long till dawn?

Elemental love

To love and not to love, like rain,
to let the love run through
the earth and yet remain
between us two:
my clouds of love are gathered and break in slow tears
whenever cold confronts them, keenly blown from your
despairs

To love and not to love, like sun,
to let the love-beams burn
and cherish life-buds new begun
to swell and yearn:
my particles of love keep recreating light
reflecting and rejoicing around star and satellite.

To love and not to love, like air,
not needing to be seen
but present everywhere
without, within:
so breathe me in and fill your every cell with love
and breathe me out, impurities of being to remove.

To love and not to love like god,
his angels and all saints;
To love for only good
without restraints:
love, entering dark night is lost not comprehended,
does of itself ignite, true light of life and self transcended.

Islam

min
a
ret
place
of
fire
pharos
beacon
light
beckoning
the faithful
five times
a day
on and off
flashing
and
filtered
through carved
mashrabeya
of the night

purifies
mind's light
of reason
lifts
pointed
slender
stem
of feeling

cleaves
the sky
spiralling
like smoke

above the domed
house of gathered
living

above the court
yard
of cleansed hearts
above pillared
terraces of prayer

where forehead
stoops to dent
hallowed dust
and palms open
holding nothing back

through minaret
like lightning
conducted

flames
one
true thought
ALLAH

Food

Jesus said 'my meat is to do the will of my Father.'
JOHN 4:34

Another's *will* is my meat.
all the food that I eat
is *will* I accept for my own;

though I screamed with colic
in pain and in panic
for days and nights of rebellion.

The steel spoon threatens;
spoonfed, the gluttons
take any kind of medicine;

I must starve rather
than swallow the Other
whose will is my destruction.

Fruits here and there stolen
are strictly forbidden
in case they prove to be poison;

I must risk dying
or stomach the lying
that feeds me on the inhuman.

In Egypt the slaves
knew how the flesh craves
when the *will* is deprived of freedom;

my bread shall be stones;
my teeth and my bones
shall forcefully enter the kingdom.

The salt desert water
has not lost its savour
preserves my will from corruption;

let his will be my meat
that builds me complete
a body for resurrection.

The Rebel

In the name of study
and for the sake of knowledge
we encourage children
to press flowers
pin butterflies

In the name of study
and for the sake of knowledge
brilliant scientists
experiment with animals
pin-point the stuff of life

'How dare you press a snowdrop,
a living thing?'
wept the child, little knowing
how soon she would herself be pressed
in the hard-backed pages
of Education

But when I observe
how much wire
and what miles of iron and steel
are required
to pin down the human spirit
and that it still flowers –

I take hope
and move paper wings
open desiccated petals
in the love released
by this tiny rebel

The New Gestalt

the liberated woman looks at the lotus

> *It is virtually impossible for the well-educated person to*
> *think of himself as a complex, interlocking series of*
> *scintillating and pulsating energy-fields*
>
> GEORGE MEEK, quoted by Lyall Watson in
> *The Romeo Error*

The Renaissance is over:
    we can un-cling the fingers of causation
    and unbend the thumbs of organisation;
    we can leave that dark woodscape of hierarchies,
    input, output, dialectic,
    pseudo-Socratic computation,
    classical classification,
    caesarian sections,
    absence of error as highest truth.

The Renaissance is over:
    we are in transit in the back of beyond;
    the world has put out its soul
    and waits for the New Enlightenment:
        the unblinding and release of sight,
        undogmatic dance with both hands free,
        movement in open space towards the future
        towards Buddha-Compassion
        Christ-Coming –

as we leave the Self we have owned
up in the treetops
on its huge thick trunk of objectivity
and dare to jump free
into what new creature!

The Renaissance is over:
    with Man as measurer,
    Platonic myths of divide and rule,
    feasibility studies in how to be human
    as separate entities born to die
    but first demanding abundant rights;
    subdivisions spread and multiply
    wild cancer-cultures, exact replicas
    immortality in blue jeans
    threatened by Bluebeard with a bomb:
and all peter out at a Hayflick limit in anonymity.

The Renaissance is over:
    airy rationality, earthy self-satisfaction;
now we learn to breathe
with heartbeat and hormone,
peace beyond proving,
that which makes good and comes true
like water, fire, blood transfusion;
like Water, for it circulates constantly
between earth and sky
horizontal, vertical, spiral, mutual;
like Fire, for combustion to change us;
like Blood, unique in every person
yet transfusable, usable.

There is prophecy in pre-life,
in plant, in person,
that breaks through fear-barriers,
diversifies, intensifies,
mates, re-creates.

Let there be light:
    epiphanies, divalis, star-festivals,
    when we are trapped in our stars
    not surrendered to our situation,
    nor striving to change it
    but using it to leap
    torches to run with and transfer.

Let there be light:
    a pattern of points
    like acupuncture of airports at night,
    tabernacles, transfiguration,
    Candlemas, Easter;
our haloes, our auras, our suns, our moons

Let there be light:
    light – space – clearings in the wood;
    tantra, tantra, thread of the necklace,
    the open way, the way open
into life-in-love broken,
    open tents, open fields,
space for atonement.

Beyond appearance, beyond ideas,
beyond form or emptiness,
spectrums, circles, arcs of energy,
annunciation, initiation;
driven, descended from high Surmang
Tibetan teachings for our time,
knowledge burned, hammered, beaten
into wise gold.

See the bend of the fiddler
    from curve of chin
    to elbow and fingers in flexible firmness,
    chain of vibration;
see the mode of the monk in meditation,
    eyes and hands and brow and back
    bowed in a power circuit;
now do we see it, the new gestalt?

Do we hear and hold it?
    But who can touch the Open Way?

There is incense arising
from switched off statistics,
from sacrifice of self
to grow – not larger, but more alive.

Now comes a taste of freedom
    where women are the first to try walking,
    walking upright for peace –
how do they balance between extremes
without holding on?
    But they hold each other and dance,
    they dance on barbed wire
    where the good they make
    and the true they become
are concentrated in the camp
of daily life and death.

A mystical body of beauty
sustains cosmos and microbe;
that which sustains is chosen
    for harmony, wholeness, holiness,
the small, the open, the less,
the third who walked to Emmaus,
the fourth in the fiery furnace,
the extra senses of saints;
    it allows the world to spin
    the universe to expand
    contract into a span
    evolve in leaps and bounds,
    present, perfected,
    but apocalyptic,
kingdom of god awaiting
the touch to awake
as we enter the new gestalt.

Old folk at the funeral

We swirl around each others' funerals
    like leaves falling fast,
say 'My dear how good to see you'
    perhaps for the last
time – and memory filters through the tears –
'My dear, life was good and you were part
    of my good years.'

Hard around a winter wind blows
    against our lips.
Winter is for dying. 'See you next year'
    almost slips
out, forced back with sharp gust of doubt.

'How much older the children look – how old
while we look much as always I am told,
as when we used to meet – do you remember
    what I remember,
incident, occasion?'
(But we recognise each other
    only in imagination;
we who were caught up
    momentarily together
in eternal celebration.)

I and you:
my good was always intertwined with you.
You and I:
we know already partly what it is to die
having lived our season's summer through
and said goodbye.

We drift away, eyes water, scarves
    pulled tighter –
Leaves are few on the branches now
    and our hold is lighter.

A poem about a concrete poem

I shall make a concrete poem
a place by art designed
where the stones and sand of life
a mould may find

I shall open it by day
to the sunshine, and by night
when it will be a lighted place
where people will find light

I shall fill the place with books
with books of poetry
wherein the very self of things
speaks its reality

And through links and lines between them
seep like irrigation
waters from the deep earth
the flow of imagination

It will fertilise the thinking
and nourish into being
this intention for a concrete
poem that I am seeing

The words of the poem
are people coming in and out
who in their intermixing
will make a work of art

But the concrete of this poem
will never be quite set;
it will be for ever forming
that which isn't perfect yet

A fusion of diversity
within a new creation;
a many-sided goddess
in one ecstatic person

It is ecstasy of grace
yet concrete as I say
making personal the matters
that happen everyday

The poem making concrete
the energies of grace
which generate the personal
through shapes of sacrifice

I shall make a concrete poem
a place by art designed
where the poetry of persons
is created in kind

Buddhist lizard

camouflaged in stone and dust
breathing with a slow pulse
long absorbed in meditation

pulse of long meditation
absorbed into stone and dust
slow breathing camouflaged

stone longs for camouflage
breathing absorbs dust
meditation slows the pulse

stone pulses long
dust camouflages slowly
meditation absorbed in breathing

meditation longs for absorption
stone camouflaged by dust
breathing slowly pulses

then flick –
    the fiery
        tongue
            of enlightenment

Education and enlightenment

The teacher assesses the intellect
of every child
and allocates for it a section of knowledge
as it is divided for convenience
into separate fields
where those who enter
by degrees may settle quietly
in a neat but narrow corner
and call it a career.

Pedigrees:
no hybrid culture can be countenanced.
Physics may only come with Chemistry,
Greek with Latin, French with German.

What freak mind is this
which wants to resurrect
the energies of dissected knowledge,
holding the parts together
and like a tiger pouncing
from truth to truth?

'Where are the snows of yesteryear?'
In the philosophies of Greece
or in the tragedies?
In minerals of the earth
or the colours of Cezanne?
On the surface of the planets
or in the space within the heart?

Not this and yet not that:
in the tears that flow
from the melted snows of intellect
as each new endeavour
dazzles on a frozen pinnacle
before it cataracts to fertilise
another generation.

Life's summertime

It is not yesterday that I would have
return, to pioneer again that path
I cut. Nor care I for the aftermath
which hedges round the present life I live,
narrowing down the choices I must take
toward the future, and to my decline.
And yet without each effort now of mine
the world may be a future none can make.

I choose the sense of having loved to be
alive, and draw in fragrance from the past;
I balance amiably on present flowers
as each new moment sets another free;
and while the buzz of my intentions last
I build my honeycomb of future powers.

Poems written
in the 1980s

Fool and angel enter the city

painting by Cecil Collins

Fool and Angel wander hand in hand
beyond the city walls:
the poet is a fool at court
and angels something only fools believe in.
Both of us were both of these
in one coherent being.

Once you loved my harlequin ideas
my starry tidings.
Once you clowned beside me
cap o' bells a-jingle
pinions charged to fly.

Now you have settled in the city
I shall never enter
across the huge moat between us.
I stand chequered
by the squared portcullis:
you more distant than angels
and I merely foolish.

Future now

This poem is dedicated to my friend, inspiration and critic Brendon Thomas who, at the height of his powers, died suddenly on 27 August 1983: an exceptional person.

Teilhard de Chardin thought people could be divided
into those who say 'yes' to the future and those who say 'no'.
That was before the bomb whose existence is a negation
and now a 'yes' to the future has to be 'no'.
This world: mountain, river, prairie, ocean, city
is worth our affirmation, not for speed,
not for size, longevity, beauty or for strength
but for ideas, crucial, exceptional people,
like Coleridge who took in Helvellyn on the way
to visiting Wordsworth, twelve pens in his knapsack
a book of German poems and a cravat.

People could be divided into those who prefer the sea
and those who choose to live among trees and hills;
expansive imaginations that reach to far horizons
and secluded souls who centre inward.
Those who believe in the future ride on will-power, vision
to put to sea in ships they have built themselves
find and explore the unknown always beyond their sight
learning from experience just too late;
others lie on the beach, tide in tide out, convinced
nothing new ever happens under the sun.
Each of us is sections of everyone.

The sea is rhythm: rhythm in trees is slow but more
related to form: trees are exceptional people.
They do not have to try to prove or improve themselves
nor do they cease continual rings of growth;
they lose their leaves without any fuss, storing in roots
the sap that rises again for all it's worth;
belonging fully to earth but living also in sky
they have no death but only transformations.
The life of tide and tree conflict, contend within us;
exceptional people find a harmony,
their ebb and flow contained in onward spiral.

Mary said 'yes' to the future, possible god *and* man.
She was a very *un*-exceptional woman
who mostly suffer life in labour giving birth
to Love, which then inevitably dies
condemned by the world whose atmosphere it makes
degraded by the fear of transformation.
We need not worship the woman: she moves in tide and tree;
we need not worship the world, or even Love.
The rhythm of 'yes' and 'no' will find an ultimate form
and having found it let go and begin again.
A 'yes' to the future has to be obstinate.

Indian women at Windermere

Indian women at Windermere
why carry plastic buckets and pans
stooped and bending low
when you know
how to sail along like swans
your loads aloft as head-gear?

Oldish women in walking shores,
saris, coats and spectacles,
with wealthy westernised sons
Indians
living in modern bungalows –
how much of yourselves have you had to lose?

If I were you I would wish to be
inconspicuous yet walking tall;
no slavery
to nationality
whether in Britain or Bengal –
head high and both hands free.

Trees in winter sunlight

Leaning pale against the hill
in this long Lenten fast
tall trunks intangible
cast shadows on the slope
sinister, substantial

Shadow
more real
than substance
and the cause of this reversal:
winter.

Half-hearted sun
casts a twitch of smile
across the woods
where frost unmelted
seals the sap.

Leaning pale
against the hill
all my substance gone
heavy, sinister,
sloping, shadowy
into this hard ground,
forced
into a season of austerity.

Anthropos in the ice-age

Nothing comes between
my cottage and the moon
save the ash-tree's arms
and a mountain domed with firs.

No dint upon the snow
within my curve of hill
save robin and lapin –
a wide, white margin.

Now I appear and enter:
clothed in cottage
shaded from the moon
attend my fireside shrine.

These footsteps to the door
show *anthropos* is here
feebly warm, intelligent,
pontifical, magnificent.

Portrait of girl at the piano

I open the door
to music
rosewood from the piano
and a young girl playing
bare-thighed in her nightshirt
toes at the pedal
her hair tied back
and slanting neck inclined towards
the music she brings from
her expertise, her
casual confidence, her
imminent maturity.

Aeroplanes at night

The aeroplanes flew over in darkest space
their roar was louder heard in the hush of night
    lit up in starry outline like a
        skeleton, luminous, heading westward.

They keep formation, each one above the next
direction, speed, together in perfect time
    but only light-shape, trav'lling sound-stream
        sensible, all the construction hidden.

A pattern lit by love as it shows me up
is all that can be seen of my voyaging
    when tedious body weight and daily
        selfhood is lost in surrounding darkness.

And you, who fly with me, alongside but high
above the earth to destiny ever dark –
    the keeping course our only order –
        light answers light, nor do engines falter.

Holyrood park at night

Snow and solo, Holyrood park at night
flakes so brittle footsteps can press no print
    sky reflects the earthly pallor
        shadows of evening are blanched of darkness

Star nor moon, no break in the haze of white
outline none to sharpen the lion crag
    wide terrain of hill and parkland
        empty of creature beside my walking

Round the frozen loch sleep the ruffled swans
geese and lesser fowl in their sheltering
    dogs and humans huddle safely
        lights of the city for hibernation

Days are dark in winter and nights are pale
blankly folded into each other's sphere
    even gulls are muffled, humbled
        silently I alone travel forward

Far ahead I see by the gate the trees
hardened branches blurred by the pallid light
    nearly home I find beneath them
        circles of softness where earth is warmer

Friends grow distant lost in their own distress
each of us alone bears what winter brings
   stiffened frosted leafless upright
      yet unawares we make fonder patches

From *Shadows from the Greater Hill*

April 16th – transplanted

Trees do not grow for three or four years
after being transplanted;
they settle their roots.

These trees in the park
are large to have been uprooted.
The younger the tree
the quicker it settles and grows;
so I am told.

My experience is different:
roots were dragging me under.
I could not grow for the heavy clinging.

Transplanted now
I am lifted, winging
weightless almost.

My growing is to shed
all that holds me down.

I grow stems of thought
to flower as poems.

July 11th – Tête à Tête

Just where they fell
sprawled in the park
on sunlit grass
a bike, a boy, a girl
in black, white and steel.

It is evening;
they do not move for an hour;

their shadows move.

The boy and girl converse
heads together, feet apart.
The bicycle is silent.

August 3rd – dawn winds

The hill is tossing high frail wisps of
rosy cloud to glide in steady gale
along a turquoise sky around above the
perpendicular and slightly askew columns
above the triangular gap
between crown and crag.

The moon full at midnight
is now high and faded
almost a lazy eyelid
day's eye opening
or night's eye closing.

Birds chase and ride the wind
reeling wheeling
aware that in a moment
ordinary flight of day will have to be resumed.

The hawk alone is steady
keeps position despite the gale
to pinpoint a victim

and far below
grasses tinge in flower:
harebell, yarrow, lady's yellow bedstraw
among the rangy thistles and fatted doves.

December 24th – Apollo in the north

Apollo winters here,
strings his lyre like stars
through clouds, like swans
brightened in the wind;
practises his geometries
scaled to our particulars:
arcs, crags, promontories.

A coiled constricted formula
translated into sections of our landscape,
our city-weathered hill,
reduced yet refined
from Delphic drama, grandeur
or golden Minoan harmony;
his circles here, triangles,
his proportions re-coded
in our alpha rock,
our liquid sky, diagonal,
and huge, cold, omega, winter nights.

January 1st – time made new

We have crossed the threshold
into time made new.
We make it new by stepping
bravely from the familiar
to proceed into a circle
narrower but higher
bearing with us
what we can
all that ringed us what we are
but opening this horizon
in each other
for our neighbour
by the truth of our endeavour.

January 5th – Turner water-colours

As daylight dims the stars
so consciousness is wakeful over dreams.

Turner's water-colours
are not exposed to view
except in Scotland's
month of darkness
when no strong light destroys them.

Winter discovers
what summer hides:
dreams, ancient magic,
fragile water-colour feelings.

Dreams

We enter each other's dreams
by way of the flesh.
It may takes years of unsevered love
before we dream of each other.

In dreams there is no divorce.
In mine you are always taking part
and it's never any surprise.
You are young in my dreams,
young, and you simply belong.

No one can take my place
in dreaming of you.

Nocturne Lewis

It is raining on Lewis in the night;
darkness has brimmed over the hills
spilling upon the moor
and dropping into circles of inland sea.

Last night the moon was wildly shed
by mountain and cloud to reveal a sheer
countenance at the window
and blending with the water in bright festoons

but tonight the dark is raining on Lewis
on the black-house with its hunched thatch
on battered abandoned buses
derelict cars and stacks of murky peat.

Boats are plying under the rain
and enormous eels under the boats
and fishing nets are lifted
up and under the tide like diving birds.

For thousands of years of nights the stones
have loomed in lonely communion
beneath the moon, the rain,
ritually aloof, cleansed and illumined

and the white schist of my lasting self
safe and awake yet exposed to love –
its darkness and shafts of light –
takes up position in line with primeval wisdom.

The dhobi's dog

Dhobi ka kutta na ghar ka na ghat ka
The washerman's dog belongs neither to house nor
riverside, Urdu proverb

The dhobi's dog will return from riverbank in the sun
to the house, but not lie down; to and fro he'll trot
panting, semi-wild, hither and thither recalled,
never petted, fondled, either hot or cold.
Does he belong? To whom? Dhobi-ji sends him home,
Bibi-ji won't give him room. Such is my lot.

Born and reared in India, comforted by ayah
on some cool verandah of lofty bungalow
with charpai and degchi, decanter and serahi,
enervated, dusty, the whining mosquito,
black ants and red, huge fans overhead:
when all was done and said, the British had to go.

In Scotland I froze: hands, feet, nose,
in thick uneasy clothes at dour boarding school:
a wind-resistant, dismal, stern, redoubtable,
grey-stone-wall life exemplified by rule;
embarrassed to embrace, weep, laugh, kiss:
was I of this race? from such a gene pool?

I lived in Pakistan, land of the Mussulman,
governed by the Koran. I learnt Punjabi,
dressed in shalwar, travelled to Lahore,
joined in zabur, lived on dal-chapati:
but didn't my passport say 'British, born Bombay'
however long my stay in Sialkot or Karachi?

I like the way I speak, the voice my thoughts make,
yet Scottish folk are quick to think me English.
I've lived here (sixty) years (Anderson forebears
and Glasgow Macalisters – that's buksheesh!)
Still my language finds no place, no ethnic dress or face:
I plead my special case and thus I finish.

My Indian self

Let me be
myself my
Indian self
that goes to extremes
from garland to ashes
Himalaya to desert
mango to maize

Let me wear the silks
the sandals and the gold.
Let me dip my fingers
in the bowl of desire
even here in the puritan
corners of my dwelling

Let me reclaim
myself; I cannot
be curtailed;
extravagance is my form
not my style;
intensity is how
my pulse is rated

My body is myself
however ageing;
I love the way it has borne
with me all these years
and given nothing less
than life itself to others

Happiness is tropical and
love is a house with wide verandahs.
Joy is my element:
I pass it through the test
of water, fire, air
and bring it back to earth

Uneven love

All night she sat and sewed the hem of her skirt,
tacked and stitched, measured, unpicked,
it wouldn't come even.

All night ridiculous, foolish thoughts pricked
in and out of her mind like needle and thread
but wouldn't come straight.

The soft, black wool was ruckled, gathered too thick;
hacked about, it would never hang well:
she had made a mistake.

Better to undo it all and shake it free;
better to smooth every seam from her mind
of this uneven love.

At last she put it aside, abandoned, half-done;
a waste of time; they never work out
these adaptations.

But she wakes to sudden, uneven pain in her heart
tacked and stitched, measured, unpicked,
and then abandoned.

Cry out and say

I want you to love me
love me enough
enough that it hurts
hurts and you cry
cry out say
say that you love me

Love me today
today and tomorrow
tomorrow when older
older yet fonder
fonder means deeper
deeper in love

I want you to open
open your arms
arms that defend
defend your feelings
feelings you hide
hide your sorrow

I want you to laugh
laugh at defeat
defeat despair
despair no more
more means ever
ever and after

The white stone of Lewis

Do not attempt
to lift the white stone.
It is smooth quartzite
and weighs a lifetime.

You would prove your back
could take the strain;
brave, ambitious
you could handle any challenge.

But another strength is more sustaining:
able to change and take changes
lift old habits from heavy soil
get to grips with the stone surface
of self-deception.

Let those do the heaving and shoving
who shoulder burdens they cannot manage
and set their sights on defeating others
in aimless shows of strength.

You carry the stone within you
light with humour
crystal with hope
smooth with complete integrity.

The water-carriers

A water-carrier, meeting another, asked him for some
of his water. The latter said, 'Why don't you drink your
own?' The first said, 'Give me some of your water, for
I am sick of my own.'

FARID UD-DIN ATTAR, *The Conference of the Birds*

A drop a pearl
from your cup poured
better than fountain
rain or cloud
    as my soul
    disquieted
    seeks to drink,
    so pure it flows
    through all, to sink
    or rise again,
    but never rests
    save in the valley
    of emptiness
Heavy the weight
our own life fills
I offer my cup –
it brims and spills
your thirst to slake:
    we give, we take

Girl raking hay: 1918

She laughs in the hayfield, sixteen, slight,
over her shoulder a chestnut plait,
broad-brimmed hat
and long skirt,
summer, hay day, August heat,
1918, peace not yet.

The huge hayrake is twice her size,
the hands that wield it, like lilies;
death the news,
her brother dies.
While girls all yearn for armistice
the hay falls scythed about their knees.

Elegy

Willows are growing in the lake
and larches in the shallows;
tiny stars flower in the water
and white birds float upon it;
grass and bracken shape the paths
where drovers grazed their cattle;
a tribe is buried beneath the mound
family by ancient family;
a Mabinogian hound splashes
in and out of the mere.

I stumble with my conflicting sorrows:
grief that my mother is dying
and acceptance that she would wish it.
Her courage and high adventure –
may these carry her over the lake
like shadow of cloud across it.
The wind is murmuring in the larches
and wings of sailing birds.

Among the willows my grief is growing:
this earth is shedding her slowly;
the world around shall be empty of her
but my world only more full.

In the Royal Botanic Garden, Edinburgh

after the sculptures had been removed to the new Scottish Gallery of Modern Art in John Watson's School, 1985

'That was Henry Moore's *Reclining Woman*' –
    He pointed out a shape of yellowed grass
    where the large recumbent stone
    had welcomed clamb'ring children,
    tentative caresses.
'And there stood Epstein's *Christ*
    Christian soldier-like
    sentinel of the city
    watchman who never slept.'

I turned toward the trees beside the path
where first I saw that figure,
the city spread before him;
and always, looking up,
I'd know a stab of stern respect:
he could have bowed down
to have the kingdoms of this world.

'Once a girl rose from the lily pond,
    a nymph with head inclined,
    as all below her and around
    diverse fishes glinted.'

These figures now have been transplanted,
plucked as no gardener would do,
no soil taken with them,
no attentive placement
to placate their genius.

We feel their absent presence
where once we used to meet them,
sense the exile they must know
in having left their Eden,
and the loss we find
in this unpeopled garden.

Seahood

On a headland pine trees
stand in their shadows;
around them the ocean
swirls in a thousand eyes
of light, and sings
its ageless song of worlds
and red rocks,
of diving birds and their wings
flying beneath the waves,
of tiny plants and creatures
that live because of the tide
and its wayward faithfulness.

Unthought-of happinesses
shall occur, shall become of us,
because of the seahood we enter
in each other,
the distant travels, adventures
each of us brings ashore.

Water west coast

It seems as though the principal element
from which all things derive in the west is waves
    is water, water, water, only
        water the ultimate end of substance

The quartzite vein that runs through the mountain rock
becomes a cataract in a night of rain,
    the road a river; rocks and trees are
        manifestations of water's essence

And sunshine seeps, distils from a molten core
displays through rainbow seaward in slanting rays;
    the moon is ice, is crystal hardened
        blanching the ocean and dwindling shoreline

Our very breathing knows itself born of mist;
our limbs and fingers flow into coiling streams
    whose current courses through the body
        thickens to densities when we waver

The boats, the houses, shops and the wooden pier;
the heron, oyster-catcher and dipping swan;
    the curlew's cry a floating ripple;
        water, the soul of the land and people.

Russian icons

Resurrection

The greatest feast of all:
Christ in *the Mandorla*
gold, before the ruined gates of Hell,
stretches out a hand to
Adam and Eve released
by this, his rise, his Resurrection

Icon resurrected
stripped to original
revealed, restored by removing layers
to cinnabar, ochre,
pearls on robes of heroes
under blackened paint of centuries

Horses

Florus and Laurus, saints
of herdsmen, finders of
strayed horses; from left to right see how
they gallop! The angel
rides fiery-winged, raised hands
joined by a rainbow. Eyes stare up, now

knocked into a horse-trough,
crates for potatoes, boards
for gaping windows, hacked, burnt, thrown on
the scrap heap, whence an old
secret woman scrapes them:
hers the entreaty, theirs the suff'ring

Rescue

Rescued, the feeble
cloistered in a kitchen
saved what could save: cruelly beautiful
Virgin of tenderness
who heals, who salves, healing
needs, with him who leans against her cheek

The Saviour's cheek, his brow
on Veronica's veil,
his face, his eyes, *not made with hands*, but
fallen into our hands:
fallen, himself the WAY;
the Saviour saved, plucked from the burning

Emmanuel – he is
no longer in church or
holy place, but in our safe-keeping:
child, enthroned no longer
save in our blue and gold
or pearled life of an ancient woman

Protector and prophet

Intercessor, bishop
St Nicholas, and blesser
of Russian folk in town or village;
his sword could not protect
city or holy place,
destroyed lest still they work their powers

In flame Elijah, as
Apollo charioted,
throws down his fur cape to Elisha
who takes upon himself
the prophet's fate: and now?
An old sick man keeps the disused key

Truth

Broken church, stabbed dragon,
slaughtered again they do
not die. Layer by layer we simplify,
seek our own origin,
experience destruction –
for truth, an image we rely on.

Martyrs

Dimness of the past is
too bright for the present;
faded, they draw us yet toward grace.
Put to a thousand deaths
the icons are martyred
elements dismembered, without trial

They should go by water
floated down the decades
holy image facing sun and trees:
woodwork and minerals,
gesso and artistry
returned to the source whence they derived

Elements

Enthroned, *Pantocratur*
Christ within the cosmos
infinitely blue, shows the gospel:
'Come unto me all ye,
ye workers and peasants,
whose collective labour built the churches

and now has struck then down.'
We shall all return to
Sofia in whom elements consist.
Saints and martyrs, leaders
of soviets, protest!
These images, their word, may not fail

Epistle

'to dearest Him who lives, alas, away'
G.M. HOPKINS

To 'dearest Him who lives, alas, away'
I send this letter, not in hope or thought
it may arrive, or that he might reply:
'dead letter' written as a last resort,
no communication, but report
on life within my person reaching forth
to join the polar self, from south to north.

* * *

I write to those dear ones whose lives have spoken
beyond their lives, and even into mine:
Tagore, whose *Gitanjali* was a token
of waiting slow for nascent love to shine
however poor and unprepared my shrine,
growing in consciousness without dismay,
becoming lovely in love's cosmic play.

To John MacMurray for his lucid word:
two people are a person when related;
water of faith has only to be stirred
to free the self from circumstances fated,
from depending on the very fear it hated,
until the world is interdwelt by love
and footsteps walk upon the moving wave.

* * *

George Fox, for your experience of the light
of God within us all, for the way
Christ opened hidden things and spoke outright
to your condition, and to mine today:
how silence lets us hear what he would say;
your witness against barriers of words
or wars, throughout this good world of the Lord's.

I thank you for the chance of worshipping
daily in life without need of a priest;
for men and women quietly gathering
free of dogma, rigmarole and feast;
for sign and sacrament in every least
concern or prayer, spilling from the centre
where God in us and we in God may enter.

* * *

Teilhard de Chardin, to you most of all
I write, because you satisfied my mind
by showing that it is an upward fall
toward spirit and communion of mankind
in sea and earth and universe we find;
all diversities answer their milieu
Christ – within, without, alpha and omega.

Both east and west, in science and religion
throughout your life, in travel and exile,
all opposites were in creative union:
from facts of matter spirit grew fertile
becoming more alive and volatile
until within the consciousness of Man
a new threshold of love and life began.

Not only in the past of evolution
but present in our midst to be revealed
in daily life and every least decision,
all increase and all wastage of the world,
the breathing of the body of the Lord.
To be entirely human and yet humble
leaves room enough to be entirely hopeful.

* * *

Soljhenitsyn, often to you I turn
my thoughts: centred you stand, rock of ages,
Paul-archetype: lighthouse to guard and warn
against more spreading death, our world's wages.
your Gethsemane of written pages,
while we were finding rest and ease on earth,
makes suffering the measure of our worth.

I hope you'll not lose hope, although the West
has wrapped you in its freedom, made you feel
its shapeless weight upon your shoulders pressed.
Asphyxiation is a new ordeal
designed to stifle any old ideal
of reverence for life, or candle-flame
of guttering God within each human frame.

* * *

The anchoress of Norwich, Mother Julian,
experienced nothing wrathful in God's nature
but a loving boundlessness, compassion,
like motherhood, of a sustaining nurture,
source and ground of being, in such manner
that none need feel disconsolate, deserted:
we hold each other goodly comforted.

Of him and her, the human condition,
Simone Weil probed the truth and led
the way, not avoiding grave affliction;
and Héloïse outsuffered Abelard,
for women are the battered face of God.
Men have been the Marys, women Marthas
who die unpublished, unacknowledged martyrs.

* * *

Unknown to me at first, I must confess
the master-poet, Homer, I have found . . .
though most remote from me in time and place,
like Keats, I am bewildered and spellbound
at last exploring this long-hidden ground.
Can the hand of some momentous fate
have led me thus to Homer, though so late;

as if I was not ready in my youth
to hear the song or learn the singer's art;
as if some ancient or unwelcome truth
is urgent now, would press upon my heart,
that through my efforts it might play a part
in plucking us from hubris-extinction
in making this old world Christ's new creation.

* * *

Not one of us but needs a guru now.
Where shall I find the teachers meant for me?
Are they alive? And if I meet them, how
shall I know them? And in what surety
can I submit to their authority?
No sign but the mode of contradiction,
the living body marked by crucifixion.

My present helpers are unknown to me.
Perhaps I spoke with one of them today.
'My greatest teacher is my enemy'
I heard the quiet Tibetan exiles say.
To kick against the goad: more hope that way
than if I feel no hurt within the shell
of my apparent duties performed well.

Know myself, and know with whom I'm dealing:
I am said God, who needs no predicate.
Of that great absolute I am revealing
the whole within myself in tiny part
And nothing can detract from that one whit:
I am beyond all category or sect.
I, in becoming human, am perfect.

*　*　*

And so I write to you 'my dearest him'
unknown to me and yet close to my heart.
I and Thou, sense of seraphim
enlarging me, yet pulling me apart:
refining alchemy, purest art
of transformation – let me now be changed
as our self-substances are rearranged.

And not just you and I as a couple
but others in a noossphere of love;
one teacher is another's disciple –
who is then the master, who the slave?
What can I give unless I first receive
and how receive unless I struggle free
to follow the next teacher calling me?

'The nerves sit ceremonious'

EMILY DICKINSON

Now is time for ceremony
for protocol, hush, removal of shoes,
for contemplation, breathing slowly,
spine strengthened, to distance
the turbulent heart with its woes
and reduce its cravings to silence.

Five or six have overrun
my apartment in trendy outfits –
they rifle my fridge, open my oven –
they gobble, dance, shout,
spill things, turn on music,
everything thrown about.

I meant to invite my chosen friends,
prepare a meal, sample their talk
quietly so that human sounds
are not disguised, so that weight
transforms to wit and wisecrack,
or gesture of insight.

But this I must forgo.
I deny myself any intimacy
with intruders, though
civil and douce they appear
at first: no desire, sympathy:
this bereavement is private, pure.

Regeneration

Regeneration is what counts.
Like a flower newly crushed
I'll lay aside superfluous wants
and turn the way of all plants
that look for light, however pushed
away, thrown out, displaced, torn,
I shall be centred on the sun.

Perfume is not diminished when
petals are crushed or desiccated.
Colours are as clear and clean
although leaf and stem are broken
and the plant is mutilated.
Earth accepts such limitations,
protects, restores, her creations.

Insects creep from captivity
to use the plant for their needs.
It is broken, lacks beauty,
why weep with slow pity
over withered, tangled weeds?
The huge scuttling cockroach
squats with his entourage.

The butterfly is absent now
and bees have accomplished
their work before dark. Below
ground begins renewal
of the livelihood that perished.
It is not visible. I die.
another life begins, not I.

To each love its sorrow

Gaelic, they say, they sing, they weep
has thirteen words for love
and nineteen for sorrow.

Each love brings its own
peculiar, multiple sorrows;
greens and greys
are finely distinguished;
colours flow like sounds
into each other, like lines
in a carved design, like the stream,
like raindrops at the sea's edge
plashing their shiny ripples
and running away on the tide,
like mist at the mountain cliff.

What colour shall I choose?

A song out of memory
or the face of one
who has made a long journey
or the voice of one who has suffered
and still sings.

Red, chestnut, tawny, noble,
strong, golden, true, bright,
tinctured, pure, delicate:
such is the love
that has outlived its sorrow.

Envoi

from a poem sequence on the five senses, set in Paris

Travelling now to Calais the white road
I return with poems in my load

To little *grande* isle with whose tongue
I lick my poems into shape and song

Farewell *le paysage, les boulevards*
city effusive, courteously on guard

In gallery or peddled on the street
aesthetically relentlessly élite

The elemental senses here refined
are fashioned within studios of the mind

Decorated with austere caress
formulated with soft seriousness

As now I turn from stately avenue
poems, *mes feuilles, ce sont mes bijoux*

Comme la Dame au milieu de mille fleurs
J'envoie mes poèmes à mon seul désir

The city we live in

You are on my skyline
as high as eye is lifted
nothing is beyond you

I approach and
come up against
walls
your rock defences

You bridge my extremes
lead over, across
between one level and another

I pass within the shadow
of your arches
and walk the colonnade

Crescent and high terrace
would not entice me but
for sudden vista:

statue, campanile
pearl of sea, jade of hill,
well-proportioned temple

more than these
I try the narrow steps
tunnelled wynds, wrought–iron gates

that lead me where
an inner court
holds itself secluded

In praise of the world, the flesh and the devil

Order of the snake: on the silver chalice
twines a tree as handle, with climbing serpent.
This my christening present, my Indian birthright,
sacred religion.

World our home, our habitat, where we shelter;
world we love as mother and father, giving
breath and substance, all that sustains the human:
Earth is our Heaven.

Flesh the seamless garment that clothes our person
binds us, pairs us, keeps our identity and
makes a holy trinity through relations:
born of each other.

Jesus teaches love of our enemy and
love of neighbour equal to love of self, but
self includes the shadow within; poor devil
needs our acceptance.

Fruit and river, god of the olive garden;
nothing can destroy our redemptive working
close to earth, yet spiralling upward; serpent,
sign of our wisdom.

From *Medusa Dozen*

Medusa five

The man I love has turned to stone.
He may have seen the snakes in my head.
Now he cannot look at me
or touch. He finds my serpents
dangerous, their true imagining.

Blood vessels in my brain have turned
to writhing snakes. Tensed, then dilated,
they throb and twist and stretch and hiss.
They are killed by hammering
with clubs, until I retch and cannot move.

The answer was to cut off
my head from connection to the nerves;
no messages, no sudden strike;
to knock senseless, block signals,
put the lid on iridescent serpents.

The man I love is petrified.
He never looks directly at me now
or wants to see me. He has weapons
to destroy me; but I turn
the other cheek, present my other face.

Medusa six

Self-transformation is what makes us women,
our peculiarity, defining feature.
Watch it as girl becomes mother,
as the mother adapts to
every phase of growing in her child.

As women we discover
when to let our children go
but also when to hold and protect them.
This goes on even after we die.

The witch, the wise woman,
cannot be straitlaced.
She alone in all the world
speaks and acts without fear.
She understands the ways of maturation
and is part of the spiral of creation,
its dyings and renewals.

She can hate because she loves,
destroy because she nurtures,
performs what becomes true
avoiding all charades,
appears even ugly from wearing no mask.

She transforms herself
and cannot be confined to one set of rules,
one pack of ideals.
Torture or condemn her,
neglect or crucify,
she will transfigure and
never leave her children comfortless.

Medusa eight

At this late dawn
another worn tree is felled.
Hard ground of winter
receives the weight of timber
without grumbling.

The chain-saw whines;
by dark the trunk and branches
are turned into logs:
a fire to warm no-one.
Tomorrow the ashes
will be whiter than frost.

Old man, when you died
you took with you the glamour
of your righteousness and medals.

All that I was taught
in my youth to applaud
(my praises, hero-worship)
has ended with you.

We have no complaint
when a patriarch falls –
we slaves and women,
peasants and primitives.

In our poverty and bondage
we have our special orders
and grow our own gods.

Medusa eleven

Like a volcano
savage
churned rock and foamed gases
red, compressed,
long unseen, unknown,
that surface to be stilled, cooled,
turned to stone

Rocked by gravitational force
the magma within her would tilt and swell
as tides do,
erupt again,
cluttered, scoured,
would flow

Some heroes farm her fertile slopes,
channel her fires and fluids.
They love and fear.
She makes, unmakes,
not once, but slowly,
over and over, the earth.

Chanticleer

Chanticleer
I hear
your notes
float
through dark
to wake
from dreams
demand
response
from sense

You stay
never betray
your flock
or mock
at love
or leave

I read late
in the night
I weep
until
I sleep

Then you cry
my reveille
as if a tune
for me alone

The willows and the vines

Alone in a garret and dying
    O the willows and the vines
a wise old woman is lying.
She frailly talks of Luxor
her station-wagon in California
listens for our footsteps
on the stairs and corridor
it must have been before the war

    O the willows and the vines

New Year's Eve and we're dancing
    O the willows and the vines
logs in the fire enhancing
candleray and evergreen
wine, food, music, float between
our memories and losses
as we make a merry scene
each one's skull beneath the skin

    O the willows and the vines

The *vieille dame* is ninety-one
   O the willows and the vines
in a week or two if it come,
her birthday, or will she wander
from here a little sooner?
Her mind, exact and clear,
speaks to the truth of a stranger
who calls for half an hour

   O the willows and the vines

'You are primitive,' she says
   O the willows and the vines
'How does she know?' my heart replies.
Her impending death is treasure
she offers. I stoop and gather
this diamond rough and pure
to keep in secret store
through every death that I endure

   O the willows and the vines

Coaltits at the window
    O the willows and the vines
lambs are born in the meadow
robins flit on fences
the gray and white collie prances
at words of recognition:
life devours its pretences
as the mind undoes distances

    O the willows and the vines

Parable

The tree longed for the day
when she could cease bearing fruit

year after year all her energies
went into fruit production

it was as if root and branch
stem, bud, leaf and flower

had no other talent or potential
than toiling to make fruit –

the burden of it, the weight
and the never-ending labour.

If only, thought the tree,
I could use my roots to study something in depth,

my leaves to be creative
in other ways: dance, music, poetry.

I wish I could exist for my own sake
and play my full part in global ecology.

At last the time came
when the tree was no longer fruitful

she shuddered with terrible ecstasy
knew herself essential and beautiful.

Autumn came; the tree was lightsome
shed a profusion of brilliant ideas

but the farmer was no fool:
'useless,' he decided, and felled her.

Torn

between husband and children
   children and work
      work and home
         home and the world
            the world and friends
               friends and parents
         parents and husband

between husband and work and love and
   love and money and loneliness and
      loneliness and security and travel and
         travel and children and husband

between self others elders younger
   younger weaker stronger rivals
      rivals brothers sisters cousins
         cousins relatives people self

between mind and body body and soul
   soul and health health and beauty
      beauty and business business and duty
         duty and mind your own business

between writing and reading and doing
   doing and thinking and remembering
      remembering and learning and teaching
         teaching and reading and writing

between today and tomorrow tomorrow and yesterday
yesterday and the weekend the weekend and the decade
the decade and the age the age and destiny
destiny and today

between self and mind and love and writing and
others and body and money and work and
children and beauty and loneliness and
child/self writing/body/ love/mind

torn

Rose window, Vincennes

The form of the rose is fire
wreaths of flame like tendrils
grow from the coiled heart

flame forms the heart
fiery tendrils coil
to wreath the growing rose

tendrils grow in wreaths
the heart a coil of fire
the rose a form of flame

wreath formed of fire
tendrils grown from flame
the heart of the coiled rose

the rose grows a wreath
the heart forms tendrils
that coil and flame and fire

grow flaming rose
tendrils wreath and coil
form the fiery heart

Carried away

In January 1886 Betty Mouat, an elderly spinster from Shetland, was the only passenger on The Columbine, *a clipper taking shawls to be dressed in Lerwick, when the captain was knocked overboard in a gale. The two-man crew tried unsuccessfully to rescue him in the dinghy and could not get back to the ship. Betty Mouat drifted alone for eight days and nights until the boat was washed ashore on a rocky island beach off Norway.*

Like Jonah in the whale   I found myself swallowed alive
alone in the ship's bowels   the crew gone overboard
caught in a northern gale   sailsheets ripped through their hands

I heard them thump and shout   I heard them lower the dinghy
I heard the wild sea attack   lurch and rap the vessel
the ladder fell from the hatch   sealed me into the tomb

of the cabin, darkness, damp,   everything flung around
that wasn't made fast or fixed   my head, my body, free
to be thrown and battered   until I roped and tethered myself

That was the first darkness   after I'd howled and moaned
to recognize I was doomed   no one could rescue me
my horse without rider, my ship   unlikely to finish the course

When winter light returned   most precious drops of day
I stood on a chest to look out   at the desolate wilderness
my loose-reined vessel astray   in black and swirling seas

I found the skipper's watch   hung on a nail in the cabin
wound it and set it to tell the time   as I judged by light
Time was my company   my piece of the human world

Snow and hail and rain   and spray coming down the hatch
cold and wet and my feet numb   no longer my own
I came on the skipper's jacket   to comfort my bruised bones

For lack of food and sleep   my thinking was erratic
I did what meant survival   action directed thought
hour after hour of dark   I gazed at familiar stars

The Columbine herself was alone   and about to die
was thrown and tossed and battered   and blown and shattered
                                        by breakers
unaware of her destination   helpless to make direction

I was her living heart   her questioning, conscious mind
I was the tiny, frail   accidental fragment
that made her more than flotsam   and jetsam upon the ocean

She and I were bonded   into a new-formed creature
no fish or sea-born mammal   no weapon or man-made object
together we made a new whole   woman and boat as one
lending each other a curious   immortal identity

                    *   *   *

Compass reading uncertain   I try to focus my thoughts
gather the yarn and firmly   spin the thread of my days
on the wheel the wheel the wheel   how do I keep it turning?

Moisten my lips with spray   succumb to dull starvation
draw from my stored resources   body tissue and memory
daze and dream and weep   and keep myself awake –

for asleep I will be crushed   in the sea's rough cradling
and the finest shawls ever made   bundles of them beside me
could not wrap   or protect me from that racking

The Columbine   she must practice her acrobatics now
with no applause or spectators   ride the sea bareback
let her prance dance   cavort somersault

pretend to fall to falter   to faint keep still and die
but rise again with a laugh   to perform another trick
and see it all as harmless   a jape a harlequinade

What other way to live?   What other explanation
for counterpoint of loss?   With hope and happiness
the skipper drowns   and he a seaman who could swim

a strong man   schooled by hardship and the sea
a man who seemed   as if death could have no dominion
over him, his powers   a man to be trusted

with ships for sailing   cargoes, shawls and precious knitting
a husband and father   a son and brother –
the two young men, his crew   did they make it home?

Young men grow faint   and their knees very feeble
the infirm survive   who no longer seek to
my lameness my greyness   my sadness my loneliness

* * *

and the shawls we knitted   taken to be treated
in Lerwick for the market   intricated pattern
like lace but wool   fine spun a refinement

our fingers and our tongues   talking and knitting
but no mistake made   that was not at once corrected
no idle gossip   but eager accurate

the stories we believe   the lives we spin
the relationships we weave   the loves we knit
but I somehow alone   my mother's only child

my father's only daughter   before he was drowned –
this is a sure way   to find again my father
the everlasting arms   the eternal waves

It is strange to be apart   but part of a community
as close as ours   each one related
but I am separate   and alone I sail

towards my death any moment   my death   how many days?
the waters invade the ship   will sink   how many nights?
dark   it is loud   seascape shouts with dark

no stars again tonight   shall I see the sun
once more before the end? Shall I be forgiven
for hardness of heart for pride in my talents

for keeping love ashore   not letting it drift
on the waves and be drowned   be surfaced and stranded
for holding love dry   for the deprivation?

Shall I be forgiven   for lack of indulgence
for prudence and thrift   for supporting myself
and teaching the young   and helping my neighbour?

This is my punishment   driven out to sea
sent into exile   banished by the wind
lost in the distance   floating the fathoms

taken to sea in a storm   of love in brain and hands
the sails of it torn from my holding   my body thrown
to the waves   but chained   confined   solitary
as I travel I know not where and against my will

*   *   *

Mother I love you mother where are you
mother and father I'm calling you calling
my voice can't be heard I am in the womb

let me be born as daylight returns
I am born each time I emerge through the hatch
the companionway and I see rocks a red light

today I see land land   means hope eight days old
but also danger   rocks will strike and gouge
timbers will scrape and crack   I cannot guide her

someone may see me   before I lose consciousness
I must be visible   climb on deck
lie like a seal awaiting the guns   be seen

must prove I am who I am   unwise old woman
determined child   competent clever in control
quietly me   reliable brave

no one complains of me   nor I of them
I don't want to make a fuss   why should I hope to be saved?
Why should I exist and why   why should I die?

People lift me   strong men take me
now I can faint now I can sleep   now I can drift
now I can sail away   *The Columbine* crashes and breaks

on the rocks on the island shore   the land
destroys what the sea could not   now I must
leave her   my womb tomb   my floating chrysalis

I am her soul departing   for I have arrived

Poems written
in the 1990s

Floating people

Tides are slowly encroaching on the coast
beaches disappear that we knew
seaside resorts are flooded, only spires
are seen at low tide in fear
the outline of dry land is lost and blurred.

The wise are already building boats
new designs, experiments; they learn.
Families clear out their homes.
They teach themselves the art of navigation
and seamanship, like ancient Celtic monks.

Seasons we used to know have melted
into one another; soil is salinated
wild flowers have no locality
trees forfeit their rhythms and are dwindling
only dark and light have kept their pattern.

Britons who could boast they ruled the waves
float as refugees in makeshift craft.
'Great London is no more' it is cried
and every slight hillock is a prize
for people who would stake themselves an acre.

* * *

But who will take us in, with our bundles
of books and precious heirlooms, family albums
pictures of where we lived, street, square
school, shops, the park or fields
or with our packaged rations, ragged clothes?

The empire that we lost or gave away?
The colonies we treated as our slaves?
Tribesmen made to dance for us and starve?
Chiefs we dispossessed and thought
were not our equals, swopped their land for beads?

Our whisky rivers now are sluggish, grey
no snow to sparkle in the summer corrie
neglected upland terrain is thronged
with ruins of the shielings, now repaired
by those who dread the sea and foreign lands.

* * *

Now we must rehearse and memorise
songs and stories of our ancestors
for these will be our passport at the frontiers
our pathfinders and our identity
when ports are crowded, people drowned.

Before I die I'll write down the notation
for each tune that sings in my story
even if I know only fragments.
My children will learn the missing parts
from others in the fuller harmony.

The wall and the tree

In India, when a tree is growing through a wall,
it is the wall that must come down.

KATHLEEN RAINE, *India Seen Afar*

Said the Wall to the Tree: 'You may grow close to me.
I'll give you shelter from spiteful weather.
Nothing can budge me, bend me or break me.
I stand my ground. Firmly founded
from time immemorial, I'm territorial.
I know what belongs. I keep right from wrong
and divide up the country, protecting property –
an effective sign of the Mine and Thine.
Beside me,' said the Wall, 'you never will fall.'

The seedling Tree accepted gratefully
the Wall's kind offer of effective cover
from heat or cold, wind and wild
animals. Young leaves and petals
shone in the Spring. The trunk was stretching
taller, roots down, branches wider.
Stone by stone it was seen to have grown
each year until it emerged, joyful,
in its own strength, settled in earth.

The Tree leaned over the Wall, looking beautiful,
its flowers cascading, leaves fluttering,
its roots creeping downward, deep.
At last it was clear the Wall was in peril:
'Hurry up and remove it. Do I have to prove it?
My stones are looser, my pointing and mortar
are crumbling. The Tree is pushing
me from below. It will have to go.'

The Tree bent to console the threatening Wall,
touched the stones with leaves, in winter thrown
by winds at its feet. Birds would flit
from branch to Wall and back. People
rested and talked. But then they hacked
the Tree to pieces. They knew their business.

Poetry goes through walls

Poetry goes through walls of brick
or stone or mud or any
solid, visible substance.
What's hard in that?
A slender plant can do it.

Walls of silence – they are the test –
or walls we face on parting,
the seven-walled city of loneliness,
which even Joshua and all those ram's horns sounding
could not have broken down.

Poetry goes through walls:
the insubstantial ones that cannot
have anything pinned or painted on them,
graffiti written on air.

Antigone!
No one shall ever again
be walled up alive. You made
poetry and it goes through walls.

Set loose

A company of long grey snakes
slides through child-high grassland
near Bangalore. The grasses roll
like waves but when the snakes
have passed they stand undamaged.

Children slept veiled in mosquito-nets
and on the ceiling a fan slow-whirled.
A cobra was coiled where I stood
to open the skylight, untwisting
a thin cord to let in the Indian night.
It had entered by the water-sluice
where bathtubs were emptied. Why did men
rise up from their string beds to kill it
then and there and cover it where it lay?

They came early to bury it next morning
in case a dog should eat it and fall dead
(as if they cared about the life of dogs).
It was a ritual: snakes must be killed
even while they sleep, innocently coiled.

Now I am disentangling the ropes
that open the sky, while men
and children sleep. Now I take up
the coiled serpent with its crushed head
and set it loose to ripple through the fields.

Rough bounds

Leaps and bounds as the river
as sure-footed mountain deer
as rock forms barrier

Rough and ready as hill track
as long standing drystane dyke
as stepping stones surely mark

The shallow place we cross over
the pass worn by wayfarer
marking the natural order

Bounds and bonds we shake loose
forsake or must sacrifice
on the destiny we choose

Universals of our planet
circumference to starry orbit
perfect each within its limit

Out of bounds we take the risk
questions each one has to ask
to go beyond may be our task

Boundless as in exaltation
the lark sings, or lamentation
that brooks no consolation

Silence then, free of words
forward then where is no guide
rough bounds within my head

Orpheus at Callanish

When Orpheus beached at Bernera
rafted on ocean tides
he gathered shells and bones
to orchestrate the winds.

Children ran to follow him;
in caves beside the sea
he carved his instruments
for raising melody.

At the time predestined
he walked the island moors
crossed the sound to Callanish
and struck the first chords.

A year and a day he played
nor slept nor ate nor spoke
till the great schists were placed
cross and circle marked.

What was the skill he knew
what secret tuning string?
He transformed what he heard
intensely listening.

The people gathered solemnly
amid their singing stones
where substances of life and death
are metamorphosed.

And Orpheus set sail again
the wandering magician
who built the stars on earth for us
who saw that earth is heaven.

Carmina Gadelica in Australia

Shipped out a hundred years ago
with Scottish island exiles
like them to seek its fortune,
the book was shelved in the University
of Sydney, while they farmed the Outback.

There it was deserted, dusty, unseen,
unrecognized, while they cut down trees,
raised cattle, sheep and children,
endured two world wars.

Les Murray came upon it and
slit the pages with his penknife
to read himself into a world
where poetry was the language of people,
their way with nature in its wildness
within them and without,
the tides of light and darkness
surging over grains of sand,
each fragile human being.

He cut the pages of his own locked life:
a hundred years of hardship and hardihood
far from the sea, and now a tide of words
in and out of old country and new,
a sea he could bathe in and come ashore
in himself, wild with words.

Viewpoint

Why can't they give these damn mountains
proper names? Their names are
in our language; the mountains
understand it and know each other
by these proper Gaelic names.

Why can't they be spelt so we can
pronounce them – like Ben Nevis
or Ring of Bright Water?
The spelling is the way it works
and makes everything real.

I can't remember these names:
what does 'sgurr' mean?
Steep, high, impenetrable peak
that divides our minds, our speech
and our understanding.

Here's one I can say: Ben Tee;
and here's Gleouraich, Gairich,
Spidean Mialach, Sgurr na Ciche.

(Mist and clouds are swirling
as an eagle soars and falls).

What is that range called that
you see and then it fades?
Knoydart. It means Rough Bounds:
dear, far, near, fearsome
rough bounds of our being.

Monks in black and white

Monks in black and white walk through the snow:
the silence of their order broken by the creak
their bootsteps make where snow is soft and clean
and by birds who scarcely sound their notes. A robin
sings alone to mark his territory
and clustered chaffinches sit heavily upon
snow-laden boughs. Crows and gulls mark out
the black and white with equal hunger, as deep in prayer
the monks walk silently in single file.

They pray for peace while tramping through the snow.
I, too, keep silent, watch wordless weapons speak,
oil gush, bridges explode, expensive
missiles shatter hard-won lives. We quietly hood
ourselves in cowls of privacy. We wear
the whited cassock of our liberal views, and know
how hard it is to think beyond the needs
of those we love. We lie alone at night and hope
for courage in the face of every day.

Icy swimmers

A heron has stalked here over the snow
unerringly to the river and lonely
as ever positions himself by a stump
humped as he waits.
    I follow his tracks
and watch as he stretches his neck
higher, holds it, until my presence
is a tree or bush, while water
laps the melting bank with fish:
icy swimmers.
    Working indoors
I know the heron wades there, alone
day and night, crumpled by wind
or stiffened by frost, stands
awaiting his chance. His life
depends on it – even as mine
has come to depend on the chance
of steadfastness such as his.

To my son going abroad

Abroad is the place to be in this world.
It is where we were born
and is always where we are heading.

This island is but one landing stage
on the passage-lines of the world
that voyagers know as they come to harbour.

To settle here is to nestle among the familiar
but you would explore.

You will meet subtle webs of thinking:
people who gather your thoughts
before you start to explain.

They will know your feelings too
and uncover words in their languages
for those we have hopelessly left unnamed –

and so you'll explore yourself
in that great abroad,
in heat and height and dirt and disease
and in the abundant nakedness,
revealed, of primeval earth
and its stark fragility.

If you lose your soul to explore the world,
the world will restore it again enriched
but do not lose patience:
that is the one thing necessary.

I shall practise it, too, in your absence
and expend my travelling words
plumed with it, and with love,
for your company, your comfort.

Kamakura

The bronze Daibutsu was sheltered
by a giant temple, but the wind took it.
They built another. A century later
it fell in a storm and a third time.
On the fourth attempt the sea itself arose
in grey pearly windswept silk
and swirled away the temple in its bosom.

They had covered the huge figure in plated gold
but sun and wind and rain and snow
of a thousand and one years
has polished it away.

Nothing can be attached to the Buddha
for he wants nothing.
Earthquakes cannot touch him but a flower can
or a bowl of oranges.
He is massive, exposed, silent, unmoving.
He is now. He is present. He is a house,
a mountain, an emptiness, a completion.

Sanjusangendo

This temple in Kyoto houses one thousand and one statues of the Goddess, Kannon. It was founded in 1164. There are thirty-three bays in which the life-size statues are displayed. The central statue has eleven faces and a thousand arms.

thousands file past
past the statues
statues gilded
gilded with multiple
multiple arms
arms and heads
heads for each person
person within us
us and each one

each one searches
searches her self
herself the goddess
goddess of mercy
mercy a thousand
a thousand and one
one is all
all is her own
her own beauty
beauty that's equal
equal to thousands

Not in a garden

For some the agony is not in a garden:
the voice of the priest reading aloud
could be heard above the clatter of silent eating
and commotion of private misery, as novices,
spiritually battered, won through to almost the end
of another day. It was an account by Sister Emmerich,
who fled massacre in France a century before,
telling of 'the Agony in the Garden.'
He began to shake with sobs and left the table,
his crust uneaten; in this human crush isolated,
unable to talk, write, think, dovetail poetry.

Today he'd received a letter, opened by the Jesuit Fathers,
from Robert Bridges concerning poetry:
Your theory of 'inscape' eludes me.
Pull the petals off a flower, fell an elm
and show me where 'that being indoors each one dwells.'
Gerard could not reply. He had written the one letter
permitted in a month, to reassure his mother
his health did not suffer from fasting or flagellation.
It did suffer, he did not tell her, from
'discipline of the eyes' – keeping them downcast
so as not to see the colours of the kestrel
or clouds in whorls of crimson.

He had burnt his poems: 'The Slaughter of the Innocents',
his children, his yield like the trees'.
Not remorselessly, but relentlessly, he had killed them.
Cut open a brain and where is memory?
Where is the sense of beauty and the faculty
that responds to *inscape*, – those 'dearest
freshness, deep down things' – call it by codename
grace or christ or soul or sakti or morphic
field, implicate order, individuation?

We glide in and out of our inscape
like a camera focusing and, sharp, we become
ourselves and poems sheer off our wings
like light on water, heedless, effortless,
bird in the dawn beyond the mist.

But among the olives his sweat like blood,
his friends unconscious and it went on,
hour after hour, with the cup forced to his lips
until he gave in, took in, let in, the violation
of death invading life.

What else shall be sacrificed?
Nine altars, passive, tall in solid stone,
now a ruin in stately gardens
at Fountains Abbey built right over the river;
nine altars for the Virgin, or the
three-times triple goddess, whose
name is unmentionable, it is too holy.
Deleted from history and untied from religion,
she pours her tincture, a cruse of
all that adheres yet changes and has its inscape
without paring – excess is not enough.

For some the agony is not in a garden:
for the Kurdish woman who flees to the mountains,
her children barefoot in sleet, her husband killed,
her baby pushing for birth and she stumbles
in terror. Gunmen at her back, no help,
no food or shelter. Innocents slaughtered
and woman's crucifixion to be with child,
with her children and unable to save them,
yet knowing herself appointed a Guardian of Life.

Nine altars   cut open a brain   he shook with sobs
and left the table   it went on hour after hour
in this human crush isolated   unable to save them
what else shall be sacrificed?

What more

The woman stood, her hand upon her mouth
and then she broke, stumbled, ran, ran
with her tears, arms stretched out.
He saw her dwindle, tiny, not more than
a speck, until she disappeared. The train
carried him off. At first the sudden slam
of pain was all he knew. But then –
to deal with it – he hated her. Obscene
to let her heart be torn from her like that: the shame.

To let her heart be torn from her like that?
What could she do? She bore within her body
those she loved; that is the way she's made
for nurturing, so that they unfold slowly;
no need to rip, to break her suddenly
in order to escape; rather to have
become entire themselves gradually –
now she also dwells in them. To leave
by force violates, undoes the fragile weave.

They bear each other, embody one another.
It is the human way. It is mature:
the child is also father and the mother
lies like a child asleep upon the floor
of every psyche. Woman is a door-
way open, no need to break it down.
What image is impressed for ever more?
He hated her. How could he have known?
He saw the heart torn from her. What could she have done?

Praise poem for the Borders

Air could not chance so keen so fine
on Spartan hills or on the heights
of Macchu Picchu or in Kashmir at the gate
of Paradise as here today on Lee Pen,
when last snow and first lambs
bloom in the sun
and the *Leithen*, marker of life,
throws off winter icicles
clinging to rock and twig
and laps up light with little tongues
let loose on this March morning
as if sprung forth on pilgrimage.

Turnips bestrew the muddy fields
and sleek cows dance attendance.
Lambs that were born in yesterday's blizzard
are dressed in plastic coats
and hop about to throw them off
like chicks from a broken shell.

No need to travel to Greece or Spain.
We are not led astray by Tourism.
Where would we see a flock of oyster-catchers
as they wheel over the water-meadows, and
the chaffinch in his new pink waistcoat,
ducks dabbling for nests
and the hawk alight on his post?

Where would we cross a pathway
striped with shadows of silver birch
or a bridge three hundred years old
over the river of battles, *the Tweed*,
flowing sedately among its keeps
and castles, hydros and farmyards?

Where would ponies crop daffodils
up the hill and rub their matted coats
on a solitary pair on ancient oaks?

This air this land this March marvel
this fin de siècle this newborn joy
this moment unmemorable commonplace
repeated year after year without
warning – as the white hare
rises in snow and lopes off onto the moor
and his summer lifestyle –

This is more than cars or cruises
to me, more than flights:
this is what I love.

Driving through Tweeddale

To drive through country is not to belong
and yet a sense of belonging grows
season by season, year by year. Some
horses will graze in the same meadows.
Coated in winter they droop and hang
their heads through rain and snows
but in April they put their heads together
then startle, shy, suddenly canter.

A foal spreads out asleep in the sun.
Nearby a cutter scoops up grass
and it falls like rain, green,
sweet. The foal will wake and prance.
Cattle are resting deliberately in
the mud they've made near the watering place.
Lamblife outplays a cruel April,
a hard rain, to bask in May and revel.

Two oyster-catchers nest beside the burn;
uncamouflaged they catch my eye quickly,
and a kestrel carelessly performs, turns
in his balance, keeps it, keeps it perfectly,
but I've passed before he drops. Hawthorn
is agleam in the green with lilac
and yellow broom and bluebell-patches
beside the water's silver, and silver birches.

Plovers rise and settle their crested
heads among humps and tufts,
and wagtails flicker bright-breasted
across the road. But where are the swifts
and sand martins? Sky is dull, quiesced,
solid without them, the river bereft,
for they arrived in demolishing rain and cold:
sandbanks flooded, nearly all died.

To drive through country is a kind
of treachery. My mother had a pony
at most, but ambled downhill to find
cowslips by the weir, or cycled stony
footpaths. Protected, I'm trapped inside
the car. I cannot touch. Only
I am touched. These presences flow,
groove into me deeply, even as I go.

From *Seven Valleys*

Love/Knowledge

The university: entirety
in its diversity
which to know is to be clever
to understand is to be learned
to love is to be wise.

Do we begin with the detail or with the whole?
Do we think with words or speak with thoughts?
Do we learn with logic or with emotion –
emotion, the whiteness from which we abstract
separate colours, the silence from which we utter?

He learnt the names and dates
and charted events on maps
to explore and travel in history,
unravel the stories behind the telling.

He discussed war and famine,
movements of population, the rise
and fall of kings, the
machinations of popes, the whims
of emperors, the struggle
of human beings to find a justice
between the one and the many,
an absolute and its infinite petty necessities.

One afternoon in the library he was drawn
to a book as if it called to him:
it was named a book of verse, but felt a universe.

Deep and deeper it led him
passage by passage
into the rose garden
where soil in its immensity
and tiny granularity,
every valiant stem and delicate tendril,
patterned leaf and stubborn thorn
with insects, birds, butterflies,
worms and clouds,
sun, rain and wind,
in a complicated dance of energies –
flower in the rose.

The flowering of the rose is all that matters:
material, it yet cannot be touched.

A bud of knowledge opened in him
and the petals of his mind received the dew.

Knowledge/Search

We fly above the surface of the earth
equipped to find what lies below it. We send rays
invisible and swift from a magic box.

The waves are reflected when they meet
some density and a screen displays in pulses
the heart-beat of the prey that we are hunting:

submarines – the sharks that lie in wait
for our ships in the Atlantic, ships that bring
supplies; it is an island we defend.

How is friend distinguished from the foe?
We share a common circuit and momentarily
the tuning coincides and makes response,

whereas the foe is passive, gives only
a constant echo, whose range can be measured
relative to azimuth and height.

The transmitted pulse must have the power
to stimulate an echo in the target, calculate
timings there and back again

with electronic, accurate devices
that keep up with the speed of light, in order to
wreak destruction on the hidden threat.

Detection of an enemy at night
below the sea, behind the clouds, beyond the reach
of normal human senses, faculties,

succeeds through this discriminatory system
made for use against a known aggressor, but we
continue in awareness of friends,

the unseen watch of ancestors, or those
who wait for us, surround us with their regular
responses and signallings of love.

In their sensitivity is safety:
he never thought of danger, knew himself sustained
between the arc of earth and the zenith.

Knowledge/Unity

Within the body of an aeroplane
the crew of six are welded into one.
They become a bird that soars and sees
its prey, that wings and, rising, weighs
along the currents of the wind.
Like cells within a single brain
they interact to navigate the skies.

The captain, pilot and decision-maker,
a second pilot ready at his shoulder,
maintained by the flight-engineer,
informed by the radio operator,
defended by men on the guns,
directed by the bomber-navigator –
each one entrusts himself to every other.

To know and do what is alone his task,
to judge when or not to take a risk,
to observe the rules of each procedure
as if they were his own second nature,
to put aside all thought of other things,
to put on a uniform, a mask:
as separate, they make a single creature.

Helmeted they roar through the air
and leave behind their weariness and fear;
their Pegasus a lumbering *Wellington*
together they become Bellerophon
in shining armour riding through the skies,
as soberly against the chimaera
they pit themselves as one being, human.

Unity/Search

The story of Snow White and Rose Red:
the children listened, chose colours, painted
the happiness and sadness of the girls.

Really or imaginatively? Feelings
become colour mixed with water on paper:
from story through heart into art.

But who wrote the archetypal story?
Anonymous: the child in all of us who mourns
the losses that accompany our growing.

Who killed cock robin? The child weeps
with all the birds of the air
and death is born, a living pain in her.

On the way to school one day she finds
a dead bird, perfect, fallen from its nest. She stoops,
examines it without the least distress.

This fact of death is not the pain of death
which lurks in her and practises its part whenever
her own mortality is touched by art.

Unity/Amazement

Ends tied together to make a loop
loops folded over to make a pattern
pattern repeated to make an intertwined
chain of ends and endings
loops and loopings
patterns and patternings
repeated and reciprocated and

suddenly by a simple twist
or pulled thread released
to a single original connection

the links that made a circuit
a person, a life
a lived coherence –
love

Amazement/Detachment

'Take care' we say, although
it is no way to live
and cannot protect body or soul
from the harm active in
every good; but we trust
each other to want to stay alive.

We desire each other
to live and that desire
keeps us living; taking care
of each other renews
our own life better
than self protection.

Some almost betray us
as martyrs dragged to death
by principles or ambitions
that lead them away from
the ground everyone needs
however exalted their flying.

Death is a mocker, has
no respect for our wishes.
Those who ache to die are forced to wait.
Yet perhaps by loving
so much we bring death on –
or by loving we outwit death, dare it.

The road that in winter
brings death is benign
in summer, and battlefields now
are covered with pale orchids
and clumps of tormentil.
Fruit must fall we have laboured
so long to mature.

Amazement/Unity

Dreams desire to sleep;
in their complexity keep
us awake, and yet dissolve
before we find the salve
that would annul the dreaming,
set desire to leap
beyond itself.

Desire expects answers
to dreaming questions
but dreams, like computers,
accept no hesitations
seek nothing in return.
Desire seeks her own,
takes headstrong action.

The head has desires
and the heart has dreams;
a wishful thought inspires
fancy's unheard themes;
sleep makes a circle
increasing in tens
to reach precious zero.

A poem for Jean

'How can I enjoy it,'
she said, 'unless I know
it's good, until I prove it,
unless I undergo
the opposites that fuse it,
blow by counterblow?'

When it works it feels like play
dances like the river
merrily merrily swept along
happy to flow where we belong
until we are cast out, rejected,
obstacles we'd not expected,
unreasonable, unclever.

Who am I?
Ask it again.
The first answer is not enough,
mask of clan and name;
now to discover another truth,
a pattern that is our own.

But when we forsake the binders and markers
we are merged into the whole
with no definition from within
we grasp at any margin
that frames us visible.

Those who love us challenge us,
who do not wish to let us change,
who want us as we were. A stranger
will beckon. We follow.

You are on a quest to find
the thread you only can unwind
within the mazes of the mind
that weaves the pattern for you.

The child must follow the mother, then wait
for her to catch up. She cannot:
the child has run ahead.
The mother is left behind to watch
as colour and shape slowly emerge
or flourish and surge
and a new creature is forged
into fullness, and she is glad.

We work, try to make good,
we nurture, give essential food
to release the free form.
You shall not weary; it is well-doing;
the end is never in sight, keep going;
you need not feel alone.

Far away on your life adventure
bravely go, behold the tincture
taking shape, a crystal
to shine and reflect all and one:
love, the love is immortal.

Blake's wife

My love walked in a wild domain
I followed him as best I could
beyond the boundaries of the brain
half credible, half understood.
He hardly slept, strange music played
he wrote, dreamed, painted.

In love I pitied, helped him work
on copper plates, the ink and fire.
We cooled it down in printed books
of prophecy or soul's desire.
The lark an angel on the wing
purest line engraving.

His *spectre* visited for days
and silent brooded on the house.
I waited, made his soup, his clothes
until he found a form in chaos.
I gathered fragments he had scattered:
Job, Dante, Milton uttered.

I rocked no babies at the breast:
this child I had was child enough.
Like Mary, I was chosen, blessed
to bear this spirit through his life.
'Jerusalem in every man'
this grain of sand in Albion.

My love walked in a wild domain
I followed him as best I could
beyond the boundaries of the brain
half credible, half understood.
We turned our trials into art
hammered the work upon the heart.

The lightest snow

Flake by separate snow-flake falls
over Tintern Abbey, glades
between columns, arches, open
full moon ring of eastern window,
chimney places, staircases,
meadows spreading to the Wye
as it loops and lingers beneath
wooded hills, takes on snow.

Day is brief before the winter dark
returns. Flakes, like grace, are lit
by low pale cold sunbeams.
We are not warmed but awed by
beauty so austere. Yet the poem tells:
you will recall acts of kindness,
be captivated by a presence
never to be recaptured.
    A deep coldness.
A winter day. The lightest snow.

Shrine

Love is not a landscape we can change.
It abides within the implicate order
folded out of our sight and range
to manifest in part, in places,
to the unwithheld observer.

As continents move from the turbulent
energies we weld into firmament
of time and space, we want to arrange
the boundless, trap it and gather
up its fragments; the white tiger
is tamed, the serpent speared; danger
given a shrine, a landscape, beloved faces.

Waiting

The image is of stillness, intransitive
and yet it takes a mountain's mass
of energy to wait, with objective
or without, whether we guess
what is to come or, futureless
we're vigilant, instinctive.

We wait perpetually for future grief
yet occupy ourselves, to leave no space
for it. With it comes relief
from cramped dread; then the press
of pain, like the tide, races
in its own time against our barrier reef.

I accommodate departure and return,
make room for one to die. It is expected.
But with the loss a pattern
of attention will be changed, directed
now towards the unforeseen, an awaited
stillness in the sea, movement in mountain.

Honey

for my mother

I hate to see you eating sliced bread
and pasty honey you have to smear
from a plastic crucible, tearing back
the thin cover with inaccurate fingers

when honey used to ooze for you from the comb
to spread and share without stint, the
very bees flew for you and flowers opened
in the Spring of your country childhood

that you cannot recover as in your dreams.
Yet I see it today with your memory's eye
and you as Titania, uncrowned, but queen
of the cowslip field and the bluebell wood.

The night walking

Why does she walk about in the night,
climb out of bed and over the edge
of rail or bar, to stumble
and search and wake the sleeping?

What does her wandered mind desire
in the night that cannot be found again
and is laid to rest by day
in the stir of faces and voices?

Who does she think she is as she gropes,
falls out of bed and breaks her bones
in crying need to get out
of this place, this prison of flesh?

Where does she want to go in the night,
in the corridor, tunnel that has no end
or leads to a sleep she cannot
allow herself to succumb to?

When will it cease, this walking to nowhere?
Are her babies lost? Has her mother left her?
Brothers and sisters have gone
and the husband, depended on.

Her daylight is done. Her dark is ever.
Those she belongs with are calling her, hauling her.
Do not resist any longer:
sleep my darling, my mother.

Maiden aunts

Aunt Ella, Belle and Jane
    three sisters bright and beautiful
lived together or alone
for the men had mostly died
thousands killed, unmarried
in the First World War.
The girls they'd waited for
had no chance of a husband then
    none for Ella, Belle or Jane

Ella became a headmistress
    three sisters bright and beautiful
an excellent teacher and linguist
with influence far and wide
over pupils, her joy and pride –
and for me, her only niece,
all sorts of unwanted advice:
I was sent away to school
    because Ella's word was rule

Jane died early of cancer
three sisters bright and beautiful
her energies turned against her
finding nowhere else to go
in their wit and fun and flow.
Practical, she raised poultry
and laughed and loved poetry.
Warm and kind and sane
was my excellent aunt Jane

What can I say about Belle
three sisters bright and beautiful
the prettiest of them all?
Disappointment turned her mouth down;
she complained from dawn to sundown.
She lavished her affection
on dogs, her only children.
Born to be a perfect mother
Auntie Belle, it was denied her

Aunts Ella, Belle and Jane
three sisters bright and beautiful
I remember you all with pain
and wish you had each been given
the choice of motherhood. Even
adoption was disallowed
without a husband. You took no vow
of celibacy or religion,
your fate was to be woman

Ella, Jane and Belle
  three sisters bright and beautiful
who lived decently and well.
But then I had no cousins;
men laid down the conditions
about children, one or many
and who could not have any.
It was wasteful, bleak and cruel
  for Ella, Jane and Belle

Jane, Belle and Ella
  three sisters bright and beautiful
virginity a kind of hell,
despised, denied, rejected,
hypocritically respected.
Now we can turn this upside down,
make spinsterhood the highest crown:
let fertility now avail
  for every Ella, Jane and Belle

Nature and art

I *Kodo drummer interviewed*

I run and wrestle.
You need to be strong to drum.
To drum you use your whole body
and control your breath.
You do not get carried away
by excitement and rhythm.
You are always in control.
Without control there is no passion.
It is not a religion –
drumming is an art.

II *Gravedigger interviewed*

I was still at school when I dug my first grave.
Someone has to do it.
Mechanical digger? Over my dead body –
though my son would never let that happen.
My graves are dug to measure for each coffin:
when it is dropped dead centre
you will find a three-inch margin
and depth five-foot three:
less is disrespectful, more touches water.
Graves are exacting labour.
It is my work. I take pride in it.
It demands all my strength.

III *Film-maker interviewed*

When I've made a film I think 'never again,
never again will I go through that travail.'
But then I fear I may not make another.
Did I find happiness? I never looked for it.
I don't know what you mean.
Sorrow is more important: sorrow
for the imperfection in all we try
to do, in each film, in each
demand of beauty and of truth.

IV *Mother interviewed*

It is my life. I delight in it.
You must control your breath.
It takes all your strength.
You use your whole body.
You think 'Never again,
never again will I go through
such travail.' But then you fear
you may not have another.
Happiness? There is none
to compare: happiness
for the perfection
that has come to pass.

Conception

first poem in a sequence of four

Copernicus imagined revolutionary orbs
and their celestial movement, uniformly
circular, the axiom of astronomy; and Shelley
saw Allegra stretch out her arms to him
dead dream-child in the shore's wild foam
    where he would drown
    on 8th July, a chance storm.
Leonardo might have accurately
depicted the coil of each eddy –
    a whirlwind that would raise
    such fateful double-spiral force

Conjunction that wrought wreck, death,
collusion or collision, like the typhus
fever that killed Allegra in Venice
left alone with nuns, her last breath,
born to appear this immortal wraith.
    Poems were also written,
    stories, epics, novels, Byron
and Claire, Jane and Shelley, Mary's babies
died and Keats had died and still they
    thought of better worlds, white radiance,
    jouissance, the planetary plan of justice.

Conjugation of verbs, to be, to bide, *ich bin*,
to make a bield on earth, to conjoin
forces for good, safety, communion.
I build therefore I am. The tide
cannot erase the words he made
    or the history they were composed of
    or our guilt that beauty, even truth
should be destructive and chaotic.
Did order come with reason and scientific
    method, the *Grand Orrery*,
    logarithms, algebra and geometry?

Mars was Lord of the fifth house
and Jupiter in the ascendant;
Venus, rarely, in transit, Mercury present
across the face of the sun; clash
of humours merely, consciousness
    a word, say animal, say angel,
    messenger, energy field, electrical
or resonant, in memoriam
nowhere, the message the medium,
    where atoms dance and stars emanate,
    ideas encounter, encircle, magnificate.

In praise of libraries

from the seven part series

2
In the street of Canopus east to west
where the Dogons walked, their heads in the stars
from Gate of the Sun to gate of the Moon
the world's wisdom was scrolled and shelved.

Within Museum and Serapeum
a succession of scholars and translators,
a clutch of rulers who wanted the power
of knowledge as well as gold and battle.

Lost in fire, destroyed by burning,
mobbed by murderers, neglected, buried,
sold abroad, copied and travestied,
collected privately, scattered again –

A place for the cure of the soul in Thebes,
a place for the Law of the Jews in Egypt,
a place for algebra in Asia,
a place for the music of Greece in Rome.

Christians thought they knew the answers,
erased all temples and sacred writings.
The whim of priest or wish of Caliph
replaced mathematics and scholarship.

By bread alone we have never lived
but fed by parchment, scroll and vellum
among the fusty-heads who guard them:
chant Alexandria, Pergamum.

In the street of Canopus east and west
we'll walk like Dogons, heads in the stars,
from Gate of the Sun to Gate of the Moon
while secret wisdom-crystals shine.

One speck may lie in a book of poems,
one beam be found in a book of dreams,
physics or anthropology. The bookshelf
of history winds and waits for

Souls to catch up. See them winged,
watch them change from lead to gold.
The hidden shall be found again,
the speed of light shall be excelled.

4

The palace of Alexandria,
shaped like a *chlamys*, a widespread cloak,
opened its domains for the feast of Adonis.
Women lamented the lovely youth –
'our hair unbound
our garments untied
our breasts uncovered' –
they carried him to the shore.

And returning to the palace
the people were restored
in gymnasia, theatre,
odeon for music therapy,
platform for dreaming: all
that saves us from slavery to
the opposing emotions of pity and fear
and books, a feast of them
sheaths unbound, ribbons untied
and truth itself discovered.

6

Scrolls: hidden
in perfume jars within mountain caves;
not worth stealing for thousands of years;
not gold or silver but crumbling parchment.
The past is not priceless until the present
is worthless.

A goat-boy fell upon them by chance
and scholars of all the world
prey delicately upon them, while
wars and fires and missiles and massacres
continue as before
and *The Teacher of Righteousness*
passes through the midst of us.

7

Books, too precious to keep,
too tough to destroy, too
dangerous to trust, too
charged with truth, too
silent in face of violence, too
volatile for the screen, books
are thoughts in transit; they gather
as they go more and more rolling beauty.
Who knows who shall know?
Whom will the finger touch?

Lass o' pairts

She read while crossing the road
she crossed the road while reading
a girl in Galashiels
    read a book
and walked across the busy main street
on Saturday when the signal gave her
green for go – go across – go on –
go on reading – absorbed in her book
absorbed by the traffic and clatter
she continued, streetwised, nine or ten,
a shilpit lass, a bookish lass, *puella docta*.

At the pedestrian-crossing we usually
hurry across, apologetic at holding
back the seas of traffic – for a person.
We hardly believe it can stop for
the fragile on foot. We look both ways
to be sure, are comforted by the bleeps.
As soon as we're halfway over we know
the flow will merge behind
our red-sea miracle passage.

This child I've seen had faith
greater than Moses I'd say:
no rod, no Jehovah, just her book
(god knows what book) to divide
the waves as she heads for a land
of promise.

The book rediscovered in the future

One day in the future
a child may come across a book
and say: 'imagine being able to hold
in your hand what you read,
and carry it with you and wear it out
with your life; to pass it on
bearing your marks, your name,
written in ink, your signature:
your wave-length in letters.'

Relatively speaking

Between music and mathematics lies the comma.
Between Pythagoras and Orpheus find the point
of no return. Once crossed the pass lies
only onward to another range of equilibrium.

Play a chord and try to sing it.
You cannot. The intervals are spaced
to correspond with harmonies of tone in colour
and with rhythmic growth in plants.

By the ratio of planets to our sun,
their elliptic paths and predestined cycles
we are kept in time and season
with a precision equally applied to each
earthly creature here or deep below the sea.
A slight oscillation can destroy.

The precession of the equinoxes may have
moved a continent beneath the polar ice.
When Sirius was close to earth he rose
brighter than the moon, and still
beneath the sphinx in *son et lumière*
the desert dogs will howl.

The balance that conditions livingness
to be and to become, to be sustained,
is bound to justice, hard to estimate.
No line is marked. We have to devise it
with care, taking care, burdened with it
but at the same time leaving all to chance.

We try to manage the coincidence or
plot the births and deaths, arrange
the marriages. The counterpoint to Science
is hidden yet revealed to sense
when sense itself is in suspense.

Music is our wisdom and our word promises.
Memory is luminiferous, a trail
of particles, electric whorl, wave-field
that passes through obstructions and re-forms,
an almost logical equity within totemic circles.

Balance, place, diversity, relations,
our honky tonk, our plangeancy
our plodding on to life beyond
each death, our alternating radiances.

Scottish Education

Dipped in the river of learning – curriculum –
banked and channeled in narrow courses,
the Scottish child is held by its Alma Mater
but, like Achilles, one heel remains
unsteeped, pointedly Scottish, dry, disbelieving.

From this unindoctrinated heel, this
tenderfoot, this easily wounded patch
we have to form again the entire
body of Scottish Studies, trace its outline
and recreate the flesh of our living future.

Counting

those who count
    can count
and those who don't count
    don't

now the counters want to invent
a way of counting what can't be counted

the counters need counters
to account for the uncountable

it gets them back to square one

meanwhile those who don't count
don't count on it

they count themselves lucky

there's nothing to it really

Elegy in autumn

Rain like rays lit by pale sun
at evening by Loch Ness beneath the cedar tree
beside the Abbey fort once built by Wade
to quell the clans
                              Rain so fine
you see it only in this haze of light
that shimmers over deep water where
motor launches circle at the base
of ruined Castle Urquhart, its towers
and rowanberries, drops of blood,
blood upon the *sgian* before it's put to rest

Rain so delicate we feel it on our faces
like the brush of tears and let it rest
there for sorrow of the story, for rue
of it, for songs and valour, for
pipes and ardour, for centuries endured
of callous cruelty, for every casualty,
for dull poverty amid outrageous beauty

Rain so soft it clings like memory
of those who had to sail, starving
and dispossessed, away, the sons we long for
and girls who wove the patterns of our work
in colours of our speech, gone, gone

Rain so cold it trickles in our blood
and turns our humour to a wheeze or moan,
to leave us dour and laughterless: leaves
lost, loosed, withered, sun-struck, windswept

Rain that slants like autumn in us now.

Male and female

The boy had a trike with a
tip-up truck type rear. He
needed something to load it
with, that could be emptied out
again, pedaled from A to B.

A pile of dry leaves, windswept
under the open stair, was
just the job. He set to work
hot and happily to armful
the leaves into his container.

A little girl was watching.
She seemed keen to help but
as soon as he dumped a freight
of leaves into the truck she
swooshed them out again.

He tried to explain: the object
was to move the leaves, to
carry them from where they lay,
by means of his trike, and tip
them out to make a pile elsewhere.

She didn't understand, or pretended
not to, because she went on
sabotaging his all-important task.
At last, frustrated, he shouted
at her. She recoiled, much hurt.

She had no idea it was more
than a game. Surely leaves
were for leaving? Whereas
he knew their true value as
transport fodder for his truck.

Two halves

My face is a-symmetric
　　the right side full and smiling
　　the other fierce, determined

The halves would fuse together
　　but now it seems as if
　　they accentuate their difference

Even in my eyes
　　the colours are distinct:
　　one brown, the other greener

　　　　　*　*　*

I overheard them talking:
　　I must get this work done
　　and done as best I can

And the right side was teasing:
　　it will cost you your living
　　your friends and your beloveds

The other only asked:
　　and what am I to them
　　if I have no dedication?

To which came the reply:
  the world needs its workers
  but forgets to reward them.

Reward? scoffed the left,
  Do you think I think like that?
  the work gives its consolation

What's the matter then?
  was the nonchalant rejoinder,
  some like to work, some play

    *   *   *

And some play at work
  while for others work is play –

As my two half faces say

Entwined

Guardians of India, idealists yet surgeons
or engineers, my ancestors to six generations
spent lives, sweat, tears, wives and children.
Home was a word in the heart, almost strange.

My medical grandpa: the only surviving child from eleven;
my own three siblings died. How precious I was
to my parents. My mother's passion the birds and trees,
bright flowers that bloomed in the dust *tra la*.

India and Scotland are entwined like a Kashmir shawl
round my life. The knot cannot be unravelled but
can uncoil like a snake, start up like the brain-
fever-bird that disturbs any chance of rest.

Two way

I think of India and yearn for my childhood,
my parents brave and hardworking who wilted
there, my siblings who died. Here I found
a country reserved as if promised and jilted.

How could I go back now? I made a craft
to sail through the world built from books
of poetry. A flimsy vessel, it stays afloat
through storm and piracy, between the rocks.

That's how my ancestor sailed in a paddle steamer
from Clyde to Malay, became Harbour Master.
Practical, kind, principled, tough, yet prey
to ideals, we're set to go on like that: two way.

Faded Indian bedspread

My faded Indian bedspread
threadbare and washed out
I would not exchange
for a luxurious quilt

With ancient flowering pattern
and cotton endurance
to another generation
its workaday presence

Going nowhere

Travelling to Kashmir
the delectable mountains
five days journey
through the burning plains

At Delhi a telegram
her little girl was ill
she turned back home
turned away from the hills

And I see those who give
up on promised lands
turn back because they have
the present on their hands

The Passenger

I came to the banks of the Lethe
and approached the ferryman:
I asked how much he charged
for a single, no return

I looked across the river
as it rippled in the breeze
then stepped into the rowing-boat
as he took up the oars

Your fare, he said, for crossing
in this weather, on this night
is your last drawn breath
and your last eye-light

Will you take a poem instead:
I have one in my throat?
but it swelled there choking
with wads of paper notes

My blood it is the stream
my breath it is the wind
my body forms the boat
for the ferryman: my mind

Stoic

*to Callum Macdonald for St Valentine's day 14 February
1999 when he was in hospital prior to his death on 24
February 1999*

My dearest love's a stoic
who will endure his pain
his deepest grief, believing
nothing is in vain.

Stricken, he will ask no help;
in silence he keeps his fears;
he will suffer, nor seek relief
in anger, talk or tears.

To others he'll give counsel
wise and closely thought;
the individual, universal
entirely interwrought.

His feelings do not interfere
with judgement and good measure
for generosity runs clear
in humour, love and pleasure.

In all that's beautiful and true
of good report and pure
a stoic gives to worth its due
and love that will endure.

After Callimachus' Heraclitus

for Callum, March 1999

They speak of your death, Callum, only to sing your praises
for you worked without sparing yourself to publish the poets.
You were generous, kind, wise, utterly loyal
and only perfection could satisfy your aesthetic zeal.

But for me it is not the books, nor even *Lines Review*
that for ten years I worked on hour after hour beside you,
it's the memory of how you would come and embrace me,
the doorlamp burning, music around you
and pour me a whisky on Friday evenings.

Poems were special and hawthorn blossom and ducks on the
Tweed
and white doves and martins skimming around our heads
and difficult clues solved or new words discovered
and your telling me in Gaelic 'Come now quickly to bed.'[1]

[1] *greas ort anns an leabaidh*

Imprint

Your handwriting keeps appearing on everything I touch
my dear Tessa . . .
mo ghaol . . .
from one who loves you true
and so I believe you do even now
you have gone to shade and light.

Your old hands, large and gnarled,
would delicately hold a fine-nibbed pen
or the special editing pencil you kept
in your breast-pocket as if
a little correction might be required
unexpectedly on the pages of life
as each day's poem unfurled.

In your frailty at last you could hardly manage
your signature
and were in silent tears at the failure
but you need not have wept:
your handwriting keeps appearing and
I say your name with my brain and breath
or I hear your voice recorded within me
safely in Gaelic and English.

This is perhaps an attempt of mine at replying.
I'm writing again and again.
Your absent presence is heavy to bear
although so light.
It is almost as if I am myself
the very last book you published.

Elegy

I saw a roe-deer stepping over grass.
She bent to crop or stood to poise and raise
her head, her seeming gaze
towards me where I watched within the room;
about me, chrysostom,
a visitation from the world of gold
beyond our low threshold.

What fences has she leapt to reach the lawn,
what wire, what barriers has she overcome
to dance into this freedom?
Does she bring me an essential message
of my dead mother's passage
free into joy, delight, *our lady greensleeves*,
while her old daughter grieves?

The deer has disappeared and night has fallen.
Up on the moor each tiny plant is hidden:
woundwort and valerian.
Good mother, all you gave has now been taken –
for our sake life forsaken.
Up in the woodland trees are harbouring
small creatures on the wing.

Time and the hour

We took our rest beneath the Milky Way
clear far yet near and cool,
told tales of earthy Irish things
and old folk we had known.

In mossy woods the tracks were lined
with butter-coloured chanterelles
fluted like Mahler's singing earth
and ready for our gathering.

We climbed to where the mountain waters flowed
spreading a thin veil on sculpted rock
yet islanded midstream a tiny fir stood firm
with tormentil and melancholy thistle.

Swallows settled on the pylon wires
or swooped, escaped above us.
A robin sat to pass the damp of evening
as fallen branches were cut up for fuel.

Then we lit the fire and talked a while
and fended off our sad presentiments.
We wanted to be warm and quiet and glad
to stay amid the waterfalling round us.

Roman pavane

In Mendelssohn's Italian symphony
a minor key slowly presages
the broken lyre engraved on Keats' stone,
whose house of death below the Spanish steps
abides an altar to unresting rapture:

not only that he was, as Wilde wrote,
'a priest of beauty', but that he inspired
Severn's guardian friendship in despite
their deep disconsolation as destroys
its very pain and paralyses life.

I picked a violet's leaf from Keats' grave
to keep in green perenniel appetence
for beauty's pact with truth; and yet in Rome
I everywhere was startled by perfection
made more so by its counter-transience.

Rome will remain even if what we see
of it should pass, as long as human minds
imagine such a city, such a setting
of ideals and technicality
assembled in an alchemy of power:

designs that built the Pantheon and left
it winking to the sky; that made flesh
from marble and magnificence from dust;
the detailed working out of husbandry
in art, in thought, inhabiting the earth.

Still an altar to unresting rapture
despite the pain of deep disconsolation;
I everywhere was startled by perfection
of ideals and technicality
in art, in thought, inhabiting the earth.

Sacred city

The old makes beautiful what we sense as new
as skyline over High Street and Canongate
   in floodlit outlined shining message
      graces the vision of New Town windows

The Outlook Tower is white as a candle-stem
for Patrick Geddes gave us his sign of hope
   a look-out post, a lasting beacon
      humanly making connections earthwise

This city keeps her principles castle clear
and will not waive them casually with a nod
   to tourist, banker, student, planner,
      visitor, conference speaker, trader

We live our days in shadow and sidelong sun;
what we attempt is battered by wind and cold.
   The Old Town Geddes touched will slowly
      yield with reserve her warmer closes

We make our sacred sites by our daily work
and money cannot turn them upsides for profit.
   Neglect may leave their spirit intact
      flowing anew when discovered quietly

No need to shout and label and publicise;
no need to claim top prizes or new awards,
 compete and count and measure matter:
 rather continue in thought and wonder

The last armistice day
of the century

for William Geoffrey Walford, killed 4 November 1918
aged 22, after four years in the war (1914–18)

Who shall be your rememberer now my mother is dead,
she who adored you so briefly and yet for so long?
In ninety-six years she never forgot you and kept
your photograph beside her and within her head.

You were someone we knew and yet we never knew,
the almost-haloed one, the hero who died,
whose beauty emerges here and there in us
and yet the one we sensed we lacked and missed somehow.

I feel my mother's pain as I did when as a child
I heard her describe the things you used to say and
how peace brought the worst news in the world:
too late the eleventh hour for her, when you were killed.

Now I am left alone as guardian of your presence.
When I am gone there will be none to maintain
our loss. Yet as my mother's love is absorbed
in me, her sorrow will form a lasting inheritance.

Poems written
since the millennium

Incantation 2000

Navel stone of Caledon
marker of millennium
eye of seer, druid's tongue,
word of carlin: stand upon
this footprint made for everyone.

As pebble cast into a pool
sends ripple upon ripple
so this sacred stone will tell,
bear witness, fair or fell,
to our truth and principle.

Once as chiefs stood on Dunadd
our land and loyalty they bled,
our corn, our cattle and our gold –
whoso worked with hand or head:
crofter, hunter – Somerled.

Now we forward step once more
reclaiming those who walked before:
builder, makar, engineer,
doctor, printer, traveller,
lad o' pairts and balladeer.

A step for Scotland carved in stone
a parliament without a throne
a country each of us can own
a wisdom, knowing as we are known
a going forth and coming home.

Who among us now will work
for light that penetrates the dark
for freedom climbing like the lark
for the democratic spark –
whose the tread that fits this mark?

*for George Wyllie's millennium stone inauguration, 31 December
2000: his central stone, in a circle of stones taken from each of
Scotland's regions, has carved on it the archetypal footprint and
beside it the last line of this poem.*

Jeanne d'Arc and her Scottish guard

painting by John Duncan

Who had departed from girls they loved
from home and land in search of adventure
fostered together as friend and brother?
Jeanne d'Arc could offer no reward
to the pith and pride of her Scottish guard.

Who could see her as saint and faery
who believed her, who protected
placed upon her their minstrelsy?
Jeanne d'Arc in secret accompanied
night and day by her Scottish guard.

Vision and voices, growing passion
violence around her, silver armour
fleur de lys and a night-black charger –
Jeanne d'Arc mounted at the head
to right and to left her Scottish guard.

What if deluded, what if it ended
the powerful in fear of her burned her to death?
Fire to fire, her flame has not faded –
Jeanne d'Arc escorted heavenward
by her fiercely angelic Scottish guard.

Phoebe Traquair's angels

Phoebe Traquair (1852–1936) was an Edinburgh artist working in tapestry, embroidery, jewellery, and enamelling but also in large-scale frescoes in Edinburgh, notably in a Catholic Apostolic church, the children's hospital chapel and the music school attached to the cathedral. She was Irish, married to a Scottish scientist and aligned with the arts and crafts movement who believed that art should enhance the daily lives of the general public. Her four-panel tapestry, The Progress of the Soul, *is in the National Gallery of Scotland.*

This red-winged angel of rapture
receiver of souls after
torture, the kind that life inflicts
stitch by embroidered stitch
The Progress of the Soul.

Is this red-winged angel
from the ranks who swell
the Song School choirs
in *Benedicite omnia opera?*
Or from those who cradle
souls of dead children
in their hospital chapel?
Or one of the seraphim
frescoed in serried praise
in the Apostolic church?

Pinions. Spilled blood. Tenderness.
Restoration. *Comfort-ye*, against
all odds, against indifference:
Take courage! Be not afraid!
Yet the red of these fluted wings
is fresh-blood-bright
and swan-like in grandeur.

Tapestries of the soul; *improvisations
of spirit*, plucking the strings
sewn on linen in spiralling silks,
gold, silver, satin stitch,
sumptuous.

Who receives today's dead children
blasted by bombs dropped 'collaterally'
or left for them in markets and buses
or infiltrating their schools?
What wings could sustain or soothe,
What colour depict? What linens,
what shrouds for wrapping the remnants?

And the bodies of children who slowly die
of infestation, infection, starvation, neglect?
Stretch your hands out gently for these
and fold your violent wings.

Who receives the bombers crimsoned
with rage and despair
red-winged
O angel of rupture?
Stem-stitch, split-stitch
Triptych.

Poems in response to titles of Ossian-inspired paintings by Geoffrey MacEwen in the Scottish Poetry Library

Paintings sponsored by Callum Macdonald, commissioned by Tessa Ransford and James Coxson for the new building for the Scottish Poetry Library which opened in 1999

The Landscape of the Golden Age

deer at sunrise climb the sgurr
above the golden valley
kings of the golden river

mountain oak, rowan, pine
where water cascades over
shield of shining granite

fertile glen, abundant sea
finest horses and cattle
great hounds at heel

a long dark or a long light
land for heroic people
bound in a tribal feu

Totem and Taboo

my cup my shield my sword my field
my white-breasted woman
my son my clan my race my kin
my life my death my poem

The Warrior's Premonition

when the wind blows from the north
when the tide is full in moonlight
when a door bangs in the dark
when a stranger crosses the path
when a heron flies downstream
when a kite cries through the mist
some death will surely follow
some blood be shed

The Bone of Contention

See the huge white hound at the dark cave's mouth
who will not leave though his master is dead –
the crone will bring a bone from the deer
his master slew the day he was slain by an erring
arrow from the bow of his brother
who loved the same russet-haired girl

Steeped in honour they all must die
for they cannot live with the shame –
poor loyal dog who remains to mourn
among old grey women and men .

The Hunter's Moon

Gold torque on noble warrior
gilded path across the water
huge moon blood-red and hanging
low over timbered rafter

Hot summer on the moorland
lazy days in long grasses
flowers, dragonflies and swallows
agitated in pre-migration

Time to hunt but not for deer
time for music and lamentation
time for lust and procreation
time to seed, replenish the furrow
follow the heart, its ripe desire

The Beach of Exhausted Desire

the harp is playing, shadows falling
the highway of the sea is closing
weep no more, weep no more
leaves browning, bracken's burning,
winter lulls the season's fever
want no more, want no more
wind is keening, fiddles tuning
bring in fuel and build the fire
wake no more, wake no more

The Tomb of the Warrior

not marble mausoleum but simple cairn
not chambered labyrinth but narrow pit
too many bones
a gleaming brooch
his rusted sword and carnivorous teeth

Feasting and Song

Put on the ermine, don the plaid
skirl the pipes and batter the drum
dance and be merry
let whisky flow
it must be a wedding
youth is now
the calf has been killed
bread has been baked
fruit is gathered, juices spilled

grief turns to joy turns to joy to joy
for someone someday again somehow

In my bones

Bones in dust, dust from bones
of pre-ice-age humans;
tests discover how they fed:
mammoth, reindeer, bear, fox
salmon, seal, wild cats.

What I eat in my bones:
chocolate, pasta, tinned tomato
and a lifetime of potato;
fish, butter, bread and rice
tea, marmite, orange juice.

Drill my bones, shake the dust
nothing shows how I am fed
by poetry, music, children, friends;
paintings, letters, photographs
undetectable to those
who dig my bones millennia hence.

My chest hurts

My chest hurts when I walk fast uphill.
I keep on walking. I'm in a hurry.
Within that year
my husband was ill: anguish and dread
my husband died: grief
my mother died: numbness
I retired from my work, work of my life –
and my chest hurts when I walk
uphill   fast.

I hear it said: women have hearts
that give little warning before an attack.
Mine is warning. It hurts.
I phone the doctor and ask for a check.

The nurse at the clinic asks questions
draws blood. Pressure normal
cholesterol not abnormal
but they send me to the consultant.

In the hospital I wait
with the obese, the pallid, diseased.
I wait an hour, another.
At last my name is called.
I tell the story and
tread the mill
wired up and plugged in
yes – walk until the chest hurts.

Wait again. Summoned again.
The consultant is brief:
'Your heart is OK'.
Relieved, I ask
'but what of the pain in my chest?'
He has no idea: 'All I can say is
I find nothing wrong with your heart.'

I go home with the hurt in my chest
which is not my heart.
I have it still
when I walk fast uphill.

For Callum

a year after his death: 24.2.2000

Now sleeps the crimson petal now the white
and you sleep on, a year into your death.
The white of silence and the red of grief
like tulips lean and bow
from my vase of sorrow
whose very ache and emptiness
contains your lustre and largesse.

Hekla, the volcano, brims in flames
where once you flew in Iceland's winter war,
and ash is clouding in the atmosphere;
the great Limpopo spreads
its waters in wide floods;
from north to south and over earth
unbalance and abnormal death.

The equinox approaches, gladly finches
sing, but still the wind is crying snow.
How slowly, gaspingly does winter go.
Your love a buried root,
a constant loyal thought,
despite my sad impoverishment
provides some kind of nourishment.

Now sleeps the crimson petal of your life
but white of memory is translucent, clear
like pearls, like poems; all that we endure
is glinting in the glass
a feast, a candlemas,
for merry days and Sabbaths too,
the books you made, the love we knew.

Paper

I'm defrosting my study today
and mopping up the leakage.
I'm emptying out my old thoughts
and the work of gone decades.

Tomorrow I'll be lightened, free
de-junked of letters, files
essays, talks and storage jars
of notebooks and poems.

On the radio I hear experts
talk of things as if they were new
that were discussed and debated
long ago . . . *mutatis mutandis*

I begin to understand
why the wise keep silent:
new concoctions are insipid
and regurgitation unpleasant.

Can nothing halt this habit?
We ask many questions and
invent brilliant replies.
But the children are thinking, thinking.

Their thoughts need no paper
but go through brainwaves
cell to cell and screen to screen,
electrifying the world.

Gravity and grace

Arctic Terns at Balnakil

Arctic rhapsodist from Celestial North
or stellar emanation at speed of light
    a dancing wheel around *Polaris*
        Dubhe, Arcturus, the great, the dark one

Flier in diagonal cruciform
on angled tapering wing with festooning plumes
    indented tail your daring signal
        mackerel clouds as your chariot-bearers

Come wind come storm come darkness come Great White Bear
our navigation sure, our direction set
    from Callanish the pillars point us
        upward and northward beyond our knowledge

And every step we tread on our stony ground
reveals the elemental, the fiery pull
    from airy sky to water-lilies
        arc of your flight to translucent petal

Black your diving head into white sea spray
with blood-red beak as you rise and soar away
    like Orphic music you transpose us
        where the horizon turns earth to heaven

Fieldfare

Are you bird or butterfly, *Fieldfare*, how do you fare?

The young woman knew she knew:
you couldn't be a butterfly. Why?
Her childhood book on butterflies
was open, clear, each page in her mind's eye.
She knew each one by heart and *Fieldfare* wasn't there.

Bird then, bold and handsome, speckled breast, long tail,
berry-seeker, tree-top flocker, 'rakish', says my bird book,
'gregarious and noisy'. You sound more of a *Streetfare* to me.

Not one for quiet retreat, with burst of wing-beat
you take flight then close your wings and glide
from wood to hedge to farm to field,
as you cluster in the park for nesting conference,
enjoy your travell'ing name, your country-loving attributes.

Farewell *Fieldfare*.
I too believe in force of fields and try
to let them resonate about me.
They make my daily fare to feed, to fly, to gather,
to tell and to take in

till, after burst of wingbeat I'll fold them and glide
to 'pastures new' – as Milton saw in his mind's eye –
beyond this life's extraordinary day.

The seabirds' protest

non-violent resistance to extinction

The birds of the sea convened a parliament at St Kilda;
    from Orkney and Shetland, the Small Isles, the Outer
Hebrides they gathered one week in late summer
    when chicks could fend for themselves, though few chicks
had hatched that year or the year before or the year before.

Manx shearwaters skimmed the waves, gannets glided
    on wide wings, arctic terns soared
from the north; puffins, guillemots, razorbills and
    even a pair of albatross, who acted
as moderators. The talk was mostly of climate change
    and how it was altering the relative temperature
zones of the sea and convection currents, affecting the fish.
    The skuas shrilly denied this, squawking 'No proof'
        and then
'Climate is always changing, the earth has always moved
    and we have always managed to adapt.'

But the lack of sand-eel supply due to factory ships
    which dredge the least living thing that moves in the sea;
chemicals oozed from salmon farms; oil escaped
    from tankers and the huge disturbance of deep drilling;
the dwindling of cod and whitefish with trawlers forced to dump
    them dead in the depths again after catching them
for fear of being over quota; seals, dolphins, whales
    suffering a similar fate; submarines
prowling and fouling, prowling and fouling, prowling and
                                    fouling –

'Silence,' cried the albatross, 'Order, order!'
    The chatter and cries were tumultuous, so that none
was properly heard. 'It's time to take a vote and resolve
    on action: either we become extinct
or we leave the coasts of Scotland for good and find
    another home.' – 'We might persuade the humans
to pay attention to their seas and make new rules
    for their protection, as they have begun
to do to save their land?' With a show of a thousand wings
    it was agreed a protest must be made,
that birds of every species would gather on Arthur's Seat
    to darken the windows of the parliament
and drown with their cacophony even the grind of traffic
    even the drone of debating within the chamber.

'We'll fly around encircling them and swooping lower
    closer and closer. They'll remember Hitchcock
and become afraid!' – 'How will fear make them act
    when reason has not prevailed all these years?'
'Fear and pity for their descendants who will never
    watch a gannet diving or a puffin
landing or the arctic tern in a pearl-grey sky.'

Thus it was arranged and final flocking took place
    for three weeks in October. It was noted
in Edinburgh that the sky was black with birds from the sea.
    'Return to the waves,' the people shouted, 'or
we'll have to drive you back.' It was in vain, in vain.
    The birds continued in non-violent resistance;
they waited over the winter as one by one and then
    in their tens, in their hundreds, in their thousands they
                                        perished,
large and small, littered the parliamentary precincts
    with their delicate feathered souls and desperate beaks.

Black seas

Till all the seas run black
thick with oil
sludge with oil and
clog to death with oil
cormorants and gulls
their livid staring eyes
their beaks that turn to preen
and taste their own slow-choking death

Till along the coast
in swarms the fish die
and all that lives on fish
a burning sea
a searing land
a poisoned world
by the hate we humans never fail
to foster till we choke
as we preen our blackened feathers

White sands of the west

feed our creels

Alexander's surviving cohorts after campaigning for years
in Central Asia, yelled 'the sea! the sea!' and pranced about
like goal-scoring footballers as they threw off their trappings
and ran down to embrace the wine-dark Aegean.

Had they lighted upon Luskentyre or Valtos,
the long-white western beaches of the Uists,
Eigg's singing sands, Barra's cockle strand,
Iona's north sands or any shell-blanched *camus* in the west –
they would have known they'd reached the Tir nan og
where Ulysses set sail beyond the sunset:

Jade, turquoise, emerald, luminous, the Gaelic *glas fhairge* –
colours wildly pure that strike and change to deep gentian
as first sunset streaks then moonlight shimmers a path
directly shafted to the entrance of our spellbound hearts.

'Sea-roads of the saints' and of the Viking plunderers –
Columba's expert mariners sailed alone to bring
their tough survival skills to rock cliffs and coasts
where they built their humble citadels. Living off goats
and seagulls, sheltered by solid stone, they fished those
churning whirling waves along with seal and whale,
dolphin, and porpoise, diver, cormorant, and gannet;
they gleaned the shores along with otter, heron; they
gathered herbs and seaweeds to make medicines and
then illustrated all in gospel manuscripts of stories
from the east, transferring them into a creed or manual
on god-in-sea-nature:
 Lir, Mannanan, tide and current,
wind and storm, mountain and cloud, gulf stream and
jet stream, tectonic plates and sea-bed shifts
bless us, today, tomorrow, our going out and coming in:
destroyer and provider, send the shoals and feed our creels.

The shanty town kids of Karachi

day-outing 1968

The shanty-town kids of Karachi
that great port
had never been down to the beach
a good hour's drive from the city
where the rich
owned weekend chalets and where
giant turtles crawled up the sands
at hightide midnight in Spring
to lay their hoard-hole of eggs.

The children lived in a dusty encampment
with one water pump in heat and disease;
their parents swept the marble floors of the rich
or the airport halls
and children minded the babies while their parents
minded the babies of others.

In rags and shoeless, the shanty-town kids
eighty or more
went down to the sea one day in a hired bus.
Sheltered in a beach hut by special arrangement
we took them down to the water;
they waded in with their clothes on
soon dried again in the heat;
they frolicked and played and laughed and cried
then fed and tended we drove them back
to their hovels.

Sea-scenes from my life

the dogged sea

What did I see? A dog being drowned
black and dangly down by the harbour in Bombay.
I was five and looked out of the window.

Not long after, a cargo ship in the docks exploded.
It had been carrying dynamite packed below bales of cotton.
Everyone thought the Japs had attacked (1944).
All the rescuers rushed to the harbour
when a second explosion killed them.
Bodies were blown all over the city.

The floor-to-ceiling doors of the room I was in
fell cracking down;
servants came running, my mother came running,
I was unhurt.
My father hurried back from work expecting to find
his family dead. We were safe:
only the doors and windows blown out and
gold bars from the Mint scattered over the city.
They were laying out the dead in the hospital corridors.

The day was announced we had waited for and we steamed
away
in convoy heading for Britain, an unknown country to me.
We wept goodbye to our servants in tears, to our little
dachshunds
our ancient cat. Packed in cabins for women and children
we contracted diseases; weak and fearful lest the torpedos
attacked. At Port Said I watched from the rails as Italian
prisoners
dressed in grey, were marshalled into the hold.
I swung from the bunks and cut my lip; then fevered
with tonsilitis endured the rest of the long long trip.

The stunning cold North Sea was my new ordeal:
a shivering skinny child versus the dread rock pool.
We'd run down duckboards and throw ourselves
into that high tide over the concrete side
pitted with rain in the east wind.

Never again, I vowed, would I ever be made to swim in a
Scottish sea,
though sometimes I paddled.
One such day our dogs were stolen:
our Border Terrier and my mother's adored Jack Russell.
We never saw them again.
So dogs, so death, so the sea.

Sweet and sad

Children of India we chattered the lingo
water and dust plants and flowers
as verandah players
insect crawlers bird callers
with kindly people smelling of spice who
would squat at our level or carry us
swaying barefooted and cool

Children of India
we ran in and out with our brown-limbed friends
sat beside them on charpai or durry
yes, the chapatis slapped together
nimbly the rice juice-laden fruits
sugary tea coconut sweets

Born as survivors siblings who died
children of India we never went back
or home or where our lives began
or travelling back we were awkward and old
language slippage friends dispersed
emerging as pictures fuzzy ghostly
held in the mind for generations
in sepia light of all that was passed

Children of India we never returned
but nor did we lose that strange
intermingled scented colourful
wearied drenched dried-out tested
born to die by-gone gone by
tears in smiles good bye, gone, good bye

Homeless or homeful

Before I was ten I lived in eleven dwellings
and eleven more before I was thirty and three.
Twenty-two homes to live in and leave
in thirty years, and you ask me where I come from!

I hear of homeless immigrants and know that I know.

We rented lonely dark places, stayed with relations,
were 'paying guests' with friends or strangers
and this was in war-years, the rationing,
the making-do and managing,
waiting still and hoping times,
not quite sure and maybe if and
thankful for small mercies times
when 'home' was where we were just now,
where my mother was and where she made
what beauty that she could as best she could
and never thought it not *worthwhile*.

A garden or a picture, books, colour,
the book of nature too and always
getting rid of clutter, all we couldn't carry
and a clearing-out and placing-in of us:
our stories, self-respect, the friends
we had to leave, the memories that nobody
could share with us, our dreams, dream-houses
and our need to hold together to exist.

I've said goodbye to homes where I have worked
to make them clean and habitable.
Perhaps I was a slave to them, never ceasing
in the daily task of damming dereliction.
There is some freedom in forsaking them,
in letting run unravelled the woven toil
of years, made up of minutes, that was
tight, so coiled around me.

I alone now know about those places
which I laboured to sustain and then destroyed
by simply ceasing, moving on. What marks
of me remain will be anonymous.

Don't ask us where we come from; where we go
is more important. Yet we leave a trail,
a string of beauty, broken, that we made,
homeless yet homeful, scattered now.

Kashmir

You speak with me in dream – eastern ascetic man
commune with me whatever we seem to say
    when I ask you where you come from
        turning you look at me telling 'Kashmir'.

High land of sapphires, walnut and mulberry
whose lakes reflect the hills in their violet depths
    glaciers melt to crystal rivers
        kingfishers skim amid water lilies.

The Fisher King may dwell in the Shalimar
and we catch fire – to selve and to bear the light
    whose the face we each reflect?
        Jesus the one and the thousand thousand.

Kashmir afar I love and remember you
fine wool, fine rice, fine silk such as dreamers find
    once in life and ever long for –
        now I must rest in the bluebird's promise.

The dreams I have

The dreams I have are all of the dead
my mother and father who never fail
to encompass me wherever I'm led

The husband who loved my poems and read
them with often a believing smile
comforts my dreams although now dead

The kindly woman from Wazirabad
who helped me when the children were small
is often around wherever I'm led

Long-ago friends and Vera who fed
my mind and heart with talk and tale
appear in my dreams despite being dead

It seems as if they are free and glad
to emerge as if in answer to call
and encompass me wherever I'm led.

Spilt milk

Milk from the breast does not run dry
but overflows in quick response
to heart's need and slightest cry

A wasteful surplus in a way
but natural change of circumstance
allows a mother's milk to dry

Yet as we live until we die
whatever pain or distance
we answer every slightest cry

Demeter and Persephone
were separated by mischance
and Nature's milky sap ran dry

Without demand there's no supply
of kindness and tolerance
it was the mother's turn to cry

But as night returns to day
and earth resumes the season's dance
the milk of love does not run dry.

Of grammar and leopards

How to measure language:
in dollops, in lollops, in gulps, in
sentences of course; which course:
phonetics, syllabics, linguistics or
song, dance, teeth, breath or
phrases, gestures, leaps, pounces,
sprawls on branches, long loops
or short straights, accidentals,
occidentals, pictograms, rosetta stones,
characters, brush marks, chisel marks,
pencil, plume or scratch marks or
tongue, tongues, people and peoples.

How the child's voice speaks a word
a clear first word consciously: is it *more*
or *hot* or *roti* or *shoe* or *cow* or
non or *nini* or *merci* or *dog*?
Each one's word is unique and each
one's voice, yet language shared, given
to us, a given, not a gift. *For god's sake*
was Alistair's first word: a three in one.

To grammar language is to measure it
and work with it as if it were an element
we live in. The leopard works his whiskers
as we work words and with them tell
a fraction of what we know. The rest
is body language, *parda grammatica*,
no parsing: tawny grammar Thoreau said,
fiery summer, the way it has to be
until we merge again with wind, water,
earthy silence.

String theory

The universe is knitted out of string
that must be why we used to play 'cat's cradle'
hand to hand as children *naturally*
unravelling and ravelling the patterns
unending unbeginning in the loop
our fingers stretched to keep the needful tension

Vibrating space is bendy now and warped
according to what energy and mass
what light or dark what cavernous black
holes or wormholes too miniscule
to comprehend may happen or come around
at any time. But Time is a dimension

of the whole if whole there is in such
a fluid gas or solid interweaving
in and out above below a field that
can transform, a field of forces weak
or strong, nuclear, gravitational
electromagnetic pulling and pushing us

beyond our mind's control much more
akin to what we sense and feel and
even what we think we might believe
of angels or thought-energised-by-love
with five percent made visible, the rest
seductive dark x-static energy

Oscillating filaments spin particles
as messengers across the mind of chaos
through branes, (yes spelt like that)
and whorls of branes poised in dimensions
of their own and even in another kind
of universe we hypothetically surmise

Vibrating space is bendy now and warped
fluid gas or solid interweaving
seductive dark x-static energy
messengers across the mind of chaos
fingers stretched to keep the needful tension
a universe that's knitted out of string

Poised equilibrium

written to complement George Wyllie's sculpture,
The Cosmic Tree

Lithosphere

earth's cover
frail protector
rock hard stone crust shield
test and feel
base and heel
is it real
matter takes the weight magnetic field
Earth our spinning planet
whirling gases
meteor-trailing comet
gravity amasses
dependable
physical
mineral
daily stuff we knock against about
stability
visibility
solidity
what we all can know and never doubt

Biosphere

creature
water
living forms and flesh of every kind
animal
vegetable
renewable
regeneration spread upon the wind
never just the same
interchanging
life a dance a game
rearranging
dynamic
systemic
totemic
only relationship is real
temporal
exchangeable
excitable
it takes more than one to make a whole

Noossphere

here and there
in the air
made of mind and making mindfulness
reflection
attraction
interaction

inestimable thoughtful playfulness
we see what we imagine
capture an *idea*
transfiguration
we fail we aspire
make special
perform ritual
this is spiritual
holy ground we tread on sacred earth
archangel
save and heal
make real
transform every death into a birth

transform every death into a birth
it takes more than one to make a whole
what we all can know and never doubt

Saving the planet

something to die for

To die: to give up life for
to die for means to live for
would we want to die for what
we would not live for?

We cannot die for ourselves since death is the end of us
we cannot live for ourselves since that is absurdity
we die for what we can give and abandon generously.

Here is what we die for:
our family name and honour
our children and children's children
the principle of beauty in truth
a working mind and heart
humans who live with the planet
who thrive on thrift
who love to share and build
more life, life to die for.

Wounded dancer

the earth as holy ground

The dancer holds her breath
homo-would-be-wise walks the earth
boots up and strides the earth
which now lies inert
the dancer hurt

In throes of anti-matter we
participate in misery
while fragments of freedom
emerge from cracked ground

Out of death and dereliction
anti-death and resurrection
the dancer unbound
as we throw off our platform soles
to tread on sacred ground

Which feeds but is not consumed
burning does not burn
speaking does not denounce
providing does not denude
withers but does not perish
like rock, like grass, like air, like water,
like ideas, like love, like us, us
creatures made of stars for Earth,
planetarians for this planet
world without end amen.

Adding to favourites

What is our favourite in all creation?
Air cried, 'let there be breezes.'
Water declared for tides and wells.
Fire wanted new-found planets
but the goddess of *Earth* said 'let there be bees.'
Mother and child agreed
and the cowslip bells.

Had they but deigned

*Had they (Adam and Eve) but deigned to keep the
word of the Holy One bright in their breasts...*
    The Exeter Book, Cathedral Library, Exeter

Had they but deigned, Adam and Eve,
what common weal might have sustained
life on Earth, what blood unshed,
the tooth, the eye, the claw, the red;
pride might have died,
with losing face, with shame, disgrace.

That bright word, had it been nursed,
might have restrained the jealous brother,
saved us from our meat-making slaughter,
taught us that humans in their true nature
work together.

The snake's connivance then unneeded
a search for wisdom could have tempted
within the precincts of Holy Earth.
Men and women might have retained
that word in their breasts: illumined *love* –
had they but deigned, Adam and Eve.

Good Friday, Leipzig

Church bells keep on ringing
as I struggle with my grief:
O *Haupt voll Blut und Wunden*
as you composed it, Bach.

Nightlong translating poems
that hurt me to the bone
till frozen in my being
I fell asleep alone.
Life and death and children
our terror of rebirth:
what were you meaning, Jesus,
in that last sighing breath?

Like me, like any woman,
you sacrificed your life
but not to burden others
or to drag them down to death,
rather as a freedom
a shaking loose of bonds
that trap us in our safety
enchain us in our wrongs.

The streets are full of people
quietly on holiday
for shops are shut and markets
have put their wares away.

The sadness of children
I find it hard to see
and yet a child of sorrow
is crying still in me.
Much has been forgotten
that has formed what now I am
and what I become for others
is not subject to time.

My heartscape is sufficient
to hold and to release
what memory can't forgive
or hope rebuild in peace.
As we grope for resurrection
only one more day or
ten thousand years, it's with us,
haunts us, keeps us, everyway.

Easter in Leipzig

We came here to translate
and have been ourselves translated.
We came here to portray
and have seen ourselves portrayed.

We had rational intentions:
Leipzig and Edinburgh after all
are cities of books and music and art.
But who has created these things?
They don't appear out of the dust
or from desks of bureaucrats.

Books are the printed flesh and blood
of those whose lives have written them.
Drawings are just that: drawn
out of human bodies that know
the terror of living. Music sets free
only those, like Bach, enslaved by it.

What is it we have to forget
in order to think in new ways
and what must we always remember
in order to know who we are?
Forgetting, a kind of death,
remembering, a resurrection.

We came here to translate
and have felt ourselves translated
out of our normal lives
wrenched from our children and friends
flung into this alembic of fire
and other people's lives.

We came here to portray
and have seen ourselves portrayed
through the eyes of poets and artists.
Amazed that we want to know them
they come to life before us, emerge
from their self-imposed resignations.

As we follow the golden thread
through the labyrinth of living
there is no art without adventure
no mercy without fire, no new
life without death and back to art:
portrayal and translation.

Choices

the Goldilocks Principle

Travel light	heart is lighter
own less	room is larger
eat less	body is freer
buy less	purse is fuller
less information	head is clearer
fewer clothes	get dressed quicker
fewer books	love them truer
play CDs	listen to them
less dashing	slower living
sleep deeper	dream longer
walk further	walk around
breathe easy	feel happy

why not?
Does 'choice' mean we can choose
how to live or only the colour of
some new machine?
Goldilocks knew the golden mean
(too big too small, too hot too cold)
the value of the in-between:
that just-right balance knife-edge keen
for human equilibrium.

Alarming times

haiku round the clock

An alarm clock rang
I fell asleep again
when I woke it was too late

A clock loud ticking
in my sleeping head
I woke and thought it was a dream

Our planet changes
we know this happens
at times it changes faster

Species get knocked out
like Neanderthals
adapted to frosty woods

What sort of being
will survive, emerge
from massive global warming?

A small desert rat
with a human brain
scuttling down sandy hovel?

Or some amphibian
plying savage seas
in sun-powered frog-skin vessel?

Eco-house speaks

a garment to wear

I'm displayed as an eco-house:
not many of us yet, we are
hand-built, crafted in detail
with every latest invention
up-to-date, state of the art,
no two alike, we are each
unique, built less to last
than to be adaptable you could say,
organic you could say, breathing
you could say, a living system.

Take walls and structure:
as with clothes it is the layers than count
for warmth and we have layers
and cavities. Take roofs: the slope is
not so much to drain off the rain,
more to catch the sun in solar panels.

We keep heat in, we let damp out;
we have a circulation like the body;
we have a heart that pumps renewable
energy; we have waste disposal systems
that recycle waters, make compost,
dispose of nothing that has another use.

Light and free to live in, we stretch out
our arms in moveable positions, our
legs in swinging doors. As for windows,
they are made from whisky barrels
for letting in the subtler spirits.
We insulate
and use the ceiling space. Our kitchens
are partly garden or so it feels: herbs
growing, vegetables cooking, salads
appearing, grains and pulses heaped
in abundance; slow food, good food, languid
home-made wine, home-made bread
with its own metabolic cycle.

We have no heavy tread upon the earth;
our footprint is hardly traceable
though we are firmly grounded
and can withstand storms and
hurricanes like a reed in the river.

To live in an eco-house is to wear a garment.
We are not machines for living in, as
Le Corbusier manufactured.
Machines are too demanding;
we are intuitive and gentle;
we save you from alienation within
yourself, between yourselves and from
Nature you long to know better and
cannot avoid any longer without
tantrums; this very place, any particular
kind of place, a certain chosen milieu,
that's where we belong as eco-houses,
belong and belonging transform.

Waxwings in the park

variety is the spice of life

A flock of waxwings in the sycamore
sycamore in February in the park
park green and windswept in the city
city grey yet glistening in the east
east coast of Scotland facing Europe
Europe, Scandinavia and Siberia
Siberia which sends its icy greetings
icy greetings holding back the Spring
Spring to come, longer light and walks
walks in the park perhaps to glimpse
crested waxwings banded on the boughs.

In Scotland *occasional winter visitors*
visitors who wear distinctive colours
colourful from head to yellow tail
yellow tail and sealing-wax red tip
to every feather of the wings, wings
for chasing insects, beaks for berries
beret chestnut with the jaunty crest
pinstriped through in charcoal black
and black around the throat and blazing eye.

My eye surprises me in looking up
looking up and welcoming the migrants
migrants among our crows and starlings
our gulls accustomed to the slanting sun.

Quiet nature

Fish do not scream   although they struggle
we take the tension on the line
and slender rod bent almost double

While casting long   the peaceful hours
we tie a gaudy wanton fly
and sink it deep beneath the waters

Or modest 'brown'   on windy pools
to dance the surface playfully
in little spurts and sudden whorls

The peaceful hours   fish do not scream
we take the tension on the line
enjoy a glinting and a gleam

Reward for patience   practice, skill
with slender rod bent almost double
the quiet nature of the kill

Earth is not mocked

The earth will rise, the worm will turn
obedient to natural law
to bury us who bomb and burn

What is it we would shock and awe?
This planet that we live upon
will spin and orbit as before

Grains of sand the wind has blown
water systems running dry
soil where nothing can be grown

Poison in the land and sky
pollution in the sea, and war
launched on wilderness and city

Flood and famine, fire and fear
would surely halt us, seem to warn
who will notice, who will hear?

Grains of sand the wind has blown
the earth will rise, the worm will turn.

Carbon trading

regular verbs

I pollute you pollute he/she/it pollutes
we pollute you all pollute they pollute
in the present tense day after day
and in the past I have polluted
you have he/she/it has you all have and
they have polluted
but in the future we'll have carbon-trading:
I shall pollute and you will sell your credits
like coffee beans among baby-sitters;
they will pollute with impunity
having planted a few trees. We'll pollute
with sanitary towels nappies cleaning bleaches
aerosols chemicals our fossil-fuel burning
    our nuclear waste
our artificial clothing our trash consuming
our luxury goods and fashion-fawning
our factory-farming our throwing out
of old computers.

You and I
plod on with heavy footprint on
the earth's eroded soils and over
several times the earth's whole compass
while the poor tip-toe barefoot through
our toxic rubbish-heaps and drink
from contaminated waters breathe
our manufactured fumes beneath the
blackening clouds of global dimming.

Would that I had not you would not
he/she/it might not you all would never
dream of they would cease at once
from all declensions and conjugations
of the user-friendly active regular verb: *to pollute.*

The story of Andrew Gilligan

I'll tell you the story of Andrew Gilligan
beware – it may make your blood run chill again:
the sexed-up dossier may make you ill again
that sent our lads to be killed and to kill again
the weapons-inspectors finding nil again
the holes in the desert we dig up and fill again
the contracts for oil and rattling the till again
the public who has to, yes, pay the bill again
for spin and lies, the won'ts and the will again
the beans the media's forbidden to spill again
David Kelly they can't now grill again
little Jack Straw tumbling downhill again
sipping his bedtime Horlicks swill again
Campbell's marching on-off drill again
Blair-Bush cocks of the world's dunghill again
Gordon Brown sitting quiet and still again
Kofi Annan goes through the mill again
Robin Hood Cook with his bitter pill again
Greg Dyke waving defiant farewell again
Butler says *they all meant well* again
it looks as if no heads will roll again
we could join 'old Europe' and bring back the guillotine:
it's enough to make your blood run chill again
the too true story of Andrew Gilligan.

To the librarian

who prevented the banning of Michael Moore's Stupid
White Men *in September 2001*

Just a librarian
just a woman
you had your wits working
your five good senses
and fired-up brain

Not important
not influential
you had your profession
clear principles
standard practice

No spare time
no extra pay
no self-interest
you took some trouble
you took a position

Thank you librarian
professing professional
thoughtful person
undivided mind
action woman

Like Mairead Corrigan
like Karen Silkwood
like Veronica Guérin
like Louise Mann
like Angie Zelter
like you or me.

Prescience

ferny path above a glittering sea
beneath volcanic crag where eagles nest

complete a rabbit's entrails on our way
stripped of flesh and fur and yet intact

pointing north as we are in our walk
the stomach full of grass lies separate

what augury this means, what sudden death
what eagles swoop above our rabbit lives

on all that we have painfully digested
our little bag of membraned 'this is me'

as dragoned eyes, beaks, talons feast
on all that clothes essential inner life

we look up, out, beyond and round the crags
a waterfall is plunging to the sea

and birches hold the soil as mosses make
a tenderness for living and for dead

Transience

I tell too much, for there is much to say
complexity, how can we understand

fragility, the work it takes to build
yet one mistake can make it all collapse

incompetence much less than ignorance
not knowing what it takes, misunderstanding

that aim is not the object, and the means
are likely to usurp the place of ends

without a subtle making of conditions
in which things happen seemingly themselves

without a constant questioning of purpose
in order to achieve the unintended

to let what happens speak but careful words
encodify the silence, the accompaniment

Intervenience

green cool in the cemetery on paths
between the graves as if in dream I pass

shining lilies fallen with their vase
I, thinking nothing of it, pick them up

the vase is broken and my hand is cut
I lay it down again the way it was

to staunch the blood I gather longish grass
then set to work to weed and tend, and tend

for tending is all I now can do
tenderly intend, in death extend

once love through tying up the irises
we planted, and I clean the listening shell

I should have left the fallen lilies lying
there would have been no blood then on the grass

Quiescence

one butterfly dead in a curtain gauze
antennae like black threads and tortoiseshell wings

outspread where a rickety window prevents escape
to an unkempt garden of waving grasses and rushes

another butterfly flutters on the sill
but weakly enough for me to set it free

a host of butterflies out on the moor
and in the woods, their wings a dusky brown

almost black with orange-spotted edge
feed among bog-myrtle in the bracken

Scotch Argos, as if Jason learnt again
the shadow side of chasing for the sun

Northern Brown Argos, paler, more delicate
I'll take you for my emblem of the spirit

the kind we need to weather Scottish islands
to flutter in the light of so much sky

to value all that grows in wet and dark
and smells like woodsmoke tinged with honeysuckle

the one that dies, the one that lives
that lets itself be captured and set free

Winter, Edinburgh

my children's friends have parents now retired
and fled to Spain's apartments in the sun

* * *

down the laddered steps towards the weir
white water brown with frothing turbulence

I plod on muddy paths and watch the rocks
for dipper or the heron's flustered flight

yellow leaves hold on still to birches
tokens of the sun in dark daylight

mist, frost, a kind of underworld
or pitiless affronts from gale and sleet

head down I reach the bus stop; starlings whistle
from slatey roofs; the lumbering double decker

stops for me; passengers together
warm for the moment, settle for the ride

our streetside trees bear lights like fallen stars
caught in their branches where the leaves have gone

will we see the moon again and planets?
we never can predict and sheer surprise

at what is commonplace signals our winter
our patch of globe cold shoulder to the sun

Signs of March

This full moon shines indiscriminately
on Glasgow tonight and Edinburgh

on Arabic and Persian poets, Albanian artist,
Rwandan lady whose own radiant visage

competes with the moon, on interpreters
translators, photographers and actors

and all who work to make things work together
for good, for wine and vine-leaves filled with rice

couscous with herbs, oatcakes
and lemon cake, iced tea and water –

Our poetry addressed the moon as curved and carved
a barque to sail the inward skies of vision

but tonight there is an eclipse of the moon, for Earth
will come between and block the rays of sun

making the moon blaze like a blood orange
in dark of night until the shadow passes –

Our poets and the translators have now dispersed
but their words are travelling who knows whither

with old and young from diverse countries around
our turning earth as they follow their destiny –

In full countenance or in passing shade
the radiance floats on and comes to harbour

Autumn at Kincraig

Yellow birch leaves fall like flakes
on rooted rutted forest tracks
rain splatters
on plastic hoods among the woods.

Tawny oaks and bronzy bracken
beech leaves thickly dark and molten
as we walk
in single rank along the bank.

The living river far below
a dark brownish steady flow
then shower of sun
gently catches golden larches.

Oil pastels

sketched in *blue* with gaze beyond view
artist's image spoke to me of you
a silhouette and turned away
no eye
no feature to identify

your presence is not visible no face
nor can I recollect your voice
recognition, a photograph
I find
still out of focus in my mind

you are too much a part of me internally
for me to visualise you properly
this present absence strangely seems
the basis
for *gloria in excelsis*

Suite de poèmes

Prelude

This is our mantra
patter noster
words our voice said
phrases repeated
spoken together
older younger
matins vespers
now forgotten
as meaningless jargon
thy will be done
What will be done?
– desire of the universe
Who will do it?
through whose life
when, where, how?
Questions unanswered
answers unquestioned

Daily bread is not tomorrow's
tägliches Brot not yesterday's
carpe diem, seize the message
open-minded receive and learn –
deep in nature's curious kingdom
we arise, adapt and change
while beyond our earthly planet
our intensive brainwaves range –
Do we trespass? Who'll forgive us?
Can we forgive our trespassers:
those who would confine, prevent us
listening to the messengers?

This our mantra
our chant our dance
our gathering, feasting
our wisdom-field
pain de ce jour
draw its sustaining
strength for the step ahead –
breathe out the wastage
from mind and blood –
we will be tested
and misunderstood
yet we keep balance
hold hands with each other
dancing onward
like fireflies in darkness
shining our weakness
through the strewn minefield
of little brown Earth

Allemande

Steady now forward march
step by clichéd step *langweilig*
we want to run, to fly, to break-
dance, to climb, to mountain bike
to snowboard, surf-ride
deep-sea dive, rally drive –
Why hang about for word
from philosopher or poet?
We'll taste and see, vision blinded
addicted to the latest gadget –
Zeitgeist? Zeitgemäss?
Keeping time? Outdoing time

We put to death whoever warns us
everytime, we will not hear;
yet when Mandela speaks forgiveness
we recognise his great-heartedness;
why not Israel, why not try
another way, the other cheek
ecce homo Palestinian
why not listen, why not speak?
Words are gifts we have as humans
to sound us out and understand
yet we tie our tongues and exile
heart and sense in no-hope-land

Out of time and out of place
out of kilter the human race
running out of food and water
squandering the oil and gas
wind and sun and wave may save us
not without exacting price –
Will we respect them, realise
love:
the required sacrifice?

Courante

Down by the river
le pont d'Avignon
we float on for ever
like twigs on the water
we find our way further
and into the mid-stream
bearing a sun-beam
divided re-gathered
we dance on the ledges
caught in the sedges
skid under bridges
not fishes not midges
not dippers not divers
we are the free floaters
who cares where we're going
as long as we're flowing

Sarabande:

we *dare* say, we *can* feel
we *must* think and *these* three
in comm*u*nity, make hum*a*nity

don't *ask* much.
ex*pect* work
for *chil*dren
we *list*en
we *love* them
we *earn* them

look *af*ter us
the *un*born ones
be *there* for us
we *grow* minds
to *fly* with them
and *still* you
peck a*round* the pen

we *dare* say we're *danc*ing
sup*port* us, don't *thwart* us
we *give* the world
as *we* are given
duende
a *dest*iny
we *can* feel, we *do* think
we *dare* say, we *must* speak

Gigue

if life is a jig or a twirl or a whirl
or a neat minuet where we practise the steps
or a g-g-gavotte we do – or we're not
going to – join in the dance
while particles spin through the world
and the brain and we seldom can tell who
concocted the spell or if not interfered with
life could work some magic yet we
want to enjoy once again (ere we die)
the tune and the turn
so we take up the fiddle and step to
the middle till mopping the brow we finish
and bow

Found poem

Guardian Weekly *29.09.06, article by Ian Sample*

Planted in pages, bound in a notebook
buried in archives two hundred years
thirty-two species in tiny packets
seeds will be scattered
windblown earth-sown
evergrown

the seeds of melons –
wild melons from banks of the Orange river –
and seeds from *the tree with the crooked thorns*

Among crates of tea and bales of silk
embedded a leatherbound record book
dark specks enclosed in dusty paper
more than a thousand immigrant seeds

A chance discoverer chanced upon them
a find was found and the parcels opened –
like seeds themselves –
over water through fire and returned to earth
where shrubs have bloomed and trees have sprung
even *the tree with the crooked thorns*

Life is patient. Life can wait
when all are her agents
with space and time and the elements
seeds will be scattered
windblown, earth-sown
evergrown

A walkover

Three feet deep the leaves at Walden pond
copper gold bronze a wealth from year
to year never swept away but melted
slowly in a natural alchemy
that bears the weight of being walked upon.

A wide-scattered cover for the lawns
in our Botanic Garden copper gold
bronze a wealth from year to year swept
by winds aside and raked up into heaps
scampered over by the busy squirrels.

The mighty beech-hedge retains its leaves
within the trellis of its twining twigs.
They lose their glossy green of summertime
but stay in place while russeting to dark
illumined by the fading winter sun.

'I'm asking how to die,' my friend explained.
'What I want is a creative death.'

A transformation surely? Either hold
your leaves entwined within your trellises
or let them fall, fall singly or in gold
cascades where they will mass down deep enough
to bear the weight of being walked upon.

Blue gate

after Winifred Nicholson's painting Gate to the Isles

Blue gate alone on the hill
no attachment to fence or wall
no pathway before, behind
open to nothing and all.

Faded gate on the machair
broken, blistered your paint;
the homestead once you guarded
a heap of rubbled neglect.

Once you led to the grazing,
to garden or lazybed;
the sound of a click on the latch
brought neighbour, welcomed, fed.

Blue gate where do you open
out of and into the blue –?
We pass with a wistful smile
and let our wishes through.

The wishing tree

this lone, wind-blasted hawthorn in the wilds of Argyll is one of the few known wishing trees in Scotland
STOKES AND RODGER, The Heritage Trees

Grant me a wish O ancient thorn
Queen of the land maiden and crone
grant me a wish as I beseech

Every inch of your twisted limbs
studded encrusted pressed with coins
each one somebody's fossilised wish

What is your wish, replies the tree
as it rests in its own infirmity
Speak to me of your heart's entreaty

I wish for a Scotland green and free
a world and its peoples in harmony
where humans and creatures share the earth

I wish for seasons and climate at peace
sun air water lands and seas
an equilibrium poised alert

I wish for my poems to share a story
for my children's children's true destiny
for ripening death and rebirth

The wind was keening the tree was silent
clouds were luminous shoots were greening
blossoms were budding from every coin

Tree of the May Queen of the Light
berries of blood and blossoms white
my wishes are granted by this sign

Nort Atlantik Drift

Alan Jamieson
ISBN 1 906307 13 X HBK £15.00

NORT ATLANTIK DRIFT – the warm ocean current that runs past Shetland, keeping the climate mellower than equivalent latitudes anywhere else in the world.

For centuries Shetland's artistic tradition has been nurtured by the rhythms of the sea and the lyrical cadences of a unique dialect. Set halfway between Scotland and Norway, these North Atlantic isles have produced a distinct and vibrant culture. Robert Alan Jamieson mixes mythology, autobiography and history with photographs in a beautiful book not only for Shetlanders, but everyone who has visited, or dreams of visiting, 'Da Aald Rock'.

Slate, Sea and Sky

Norman Bissell
ISBN 1 906307 16 4 HBK £15.00

This striking combination of poems and photography creates a remarkable new soundscape and vision of Glasgow and of a land far beyond its crowded streets. From the screech of buses to the crash of waves on a windswept Hebridean shore, the poems take us on a journey from the city to an island, between two very different worlds.

Norman Bissell's evocative snapshots of people and places are beautifully illuminated by Oscar Marzaroli's stunning photographs. Some shown here for the first time, these brilliantly capture a changing Scotland in shade and light.

There is lovely work here, limpid and light, a careful simplicity of line, open to the voices of the city and the calm, restorative spaces of nature.
CATHERINE LOCKERBIE

On the Flyleaf

Ken Cockburn
ISBN 1 906307 18 0 PBK £7.99

*... Its flyleaves are thick
with poems: Sophus
Claussen, you explain,
those you didn't know
by heart and wishing,
one long-ago summer, to
travel light,*

copied in the space Calvino offered.

Art, sex, a city, a journey: Ken
Cockburn's new collection dwells
on the connection between people,
places, languages and literature.
Inspired by inscriptions, graffiti and
scribbled notes on the flyleaves of
books – Ovid, a guide book, a
superhero comic – these poems
interweave travel, home and love,
while quietly subverting notions of
standing and rank in literature.

Handling both the narrative poem
and the haiku with equal skill,
Cockburn observes and probes the
ways in which we interpret the
world with an uncluttered eye.

Fascinating well-wrought contemporary poems... exact and apparently effortless writing.
ANGUS REID

Bodywork

Dilys Rose
ISBN 1 905222 93 9 PBK £8.99

How do we feel
about the flesh that
surrounds us and
how do we deal
with the knowledge
that it will eventually
do so no more?
How do our bodies
affect our emotional, physical and
spiritual lives?

Winner of the 2006 McCash prize,
Dilys Rose's third collection of
poetry focuses on the human body
in all its glory, comedy and frailty;
on the quirks, hazards and conundrums of physiology; on
intimations of mortality – and
immortality. Rose draws fully-grown characters in a few vivid
strokes; from a body double to a
cannibal queen, their souls are
personified in a limb, affliction or
skill. These poems get under your
skin and into your bones – you'll
never look at the human body in
the same way again!

Dilys Rose exposes and illuminates humanity with scalpel sharpness... ingeniously exciting, quirky and perceptive.
JANET PAISLEY, *THE SCOTSMAN*

It's an extraordinary book, brave and unusual, full of unexpected insights and delights – and a consistent compassion, respect and reverence for the human body, in all its oddity and complexity.
CATHERINE SMITH

Let Me Dance with Your Shadow/ Dannsam Led Fhaileas

Martin MacIntyre
ISBN 1 905222 57 1 PBK £8.99

Martin MacIntyre's first collection of poetry, in both Gaelic and English, rejoices in the passion and vitality of human experience, showing a detailed observance of emotion. He draws inspiration from the past whilst emphasising the continuity and contemporising of tradition, which confronts and often consoles his concerns over the inevitable passing of time. The reader is left with a sense of finding comfort and affirmation in the richness of everyday experience.

Martin MacIntyre was winner of the 2003 Saltire Scottish First Book of the Year Award with *Ath-Aithne* and was shortlisted for the 2005 Saltire Scottish Book of the Year with *Gymnippers Diciadain*.

Stravaigin

Liz Niven
ISBN 1 905222 70 X PBK £7.99

At the core of this wide-ranging collection of poems is the notion of the Scots as a community of 'stravaigers' or wanderers within as well as beyond Scotland's borders. Liz Niven draws on a variety of resources – the history of the Scots, her personal roots and the contemporary landscape – and moves outward, through various foreign cultures and many moods, to view the world through distinctly Scottish eyes.

She often adopts a feminist perspective, sometimes with incisively satirical intent. In 'A Drunk Wumman Sittin oan a Thistle', her monologue brings new meaning to MacDiarmid's seminal poem as well as providing immense, self-effacing entertainment on the plight of contemporary Scots women. Elsewhere, Niven offers stunning lyrical verse or longer narrative poetry, always beautifully crafted and with lasting resonance.

100 Favourite Scottish Poems

Edited by Stewart Conn
ISBN 1 905222 61 0 PBK £7.99

Poems to make you laugh. Poems to make you cry. Poems to make you think. Poems to savour. Poems to read out loud. To read again, and again. Scottish poems. Old favourites. New favourites. 100 of the best.

Scotland has a long history of producing outstanding poetry. From the humblest but-and-ben to the grandest castle, the nation has a great tradition of celebration and commemoration through poetry. *100 Favourite Scottish Poems* – incorporating the top 20 best-loved poems as selected by a BBC Radio Scotland listener poll – ranges from ballads to Burns, from 'Proud Maisie' to 'The Queen of Sheba', and from 'Cuddle Doon' to 'The Jeelie Piece Song'.

Edited by Stewart Conn, poet and inaugural recipient of the Institute of Contemporary Scotland's Iain Crichton Smith Award for services to literature (2006). Published in association with the Scottish Poetry Library.

100 Favourite Scottish Poems to Read Out Loud

Edited by Gordon Jarvie
ISBN 1 906307 01 6 PBK £7.99

Poems that roll off the tongue. Poems that trip up the tongue. Poems to shout. Poems to sing. Poems to declaim. Poems that you learned at school. Poems that will stay with you forever.

Do you have a poem off by heart but always get stuck at the second verse? Can your friends and family members recite at the drop of a hat while you only have a vague memory of the poems and songs learned as a child? Or do you just want an aide-memoire to the poems you know and love? This collection includes many popular Scottish poems, from 'The Wee Cock Sparra' to 'The Four Maries', 'The Wee Kirkcudbright Centipede' to 'John Anderson My Jo'; as well as poetry by Sheena Blackhall, Norman MacCaig, Jimmy Copeland, Tom Leonard and many others.

Scots have ample opportunity to let rip with old favourites on Burns Night, St Andrew's Day, or at ceilidhs and festivals. Whatever your choice, this wide-ranging selection will give you and your audience (even if it's only your mirror) hours of pleasure and enjoyment.

Luath Press Limited
committed to publishing well written books worth reading

LUATH PRESS takes its name from Robert Burns, whose little collie Luath (*Gael.*, swift or nimble) tripped up Jean Armour at a wedding and gave him the chance to speak to the woman who was to be his wife and the abiding love of his life. Burns called one of 'The Twa Dogs' Luath after Cuchullin's hunting dog in Ossian's *Fingal*. Luath Press was established in 1981 in the heart of Burns country, and is now based a few steps up the road from Burns' first lodgings on Edinburgh's Royal Mile.

Luath offers you distinctive writing with a hint of unexpected pleasures.

Most bookshops in the UK, the US, Canada, Australia, New Zealand and parts of Europe either carry our books in stock or can order them for you. To order direct from us, please send a £sterling cheque, postal order, international money order or your credit card details (number, address of cardholder and expiry date) to us at the address below. Please add post and packing as follows: UK – £1.00 per delivery address; overseas surface mail – £2.50 per delivery address; overseas airmail – £3.50 for the first book to each delivery address, plus £1.00 for each additional book by airmail to the same address. If your order is a gift, we will happily enclose your card or message at no extra charge.

Luath Press Limited
543/2 Castlehill
The Royal Mile
Edinburgh EH1 2ND
Scotland
Telephone: 0131 225 4326 (24 hours)
Fax: 0131 225 4324
email: sales@luath.co.uk
Website: www.luath.co.uk